THE TRUTH OF THE
QUARA'N
IN THE LIGHT OF THE BIBLE

• Biola University, La Mirada, CA. Dr. Barry Cory, President. Letter of Appreciation •
• Department of the Army, Outstanding Achievement, Beyond of Service •
• Defense Language Institute, Monterey, CA. On The Spot Award •
• USAF, Captain Christopher Felt. Recognition •

THE TRUTH OF THE QUARA'N
IN THE LIGHT OF THE BIBLE

VICTOR Z. KHALIL

ReadersMagnet, LLC

The Truth Of The Quara'n In The Light Of The Bible
Copyright © 2020 by Victor Z. Khalil

Published in the United States of America
ISBN Paperback: 978-1-952896-52-1
ISBN eBook: 978-1-952896-53-8

All rights reserved. No part of this publication may be reproduced, stored in a retrieval system or transmitted in any way by any means, electronic, mechanical, photocopy, recording or otherwise without the prior permission of the author except as provided by USA copyright law.

Bible verses in English are from the King James Version.

The opinions expressed by the author are not necessarily those of ReadersMagnet, LLC.

ReadersMagnet, LLC
10620 Treena Street, Suite 230 | San Diego, California, 92131 USA
1.619.354.2643 | www.readersmagnet.com

Book design copyright © 2020 by ReadersMagnet, LLC. All rights reserved.
Cover design by Ericka Obando
Interior design by Shemaryl Tampus

CONTENTS

Foreword.................................... vii
Introduction ix

God: Allah الله 1
Isa: Jesus Christ عيسى - يسوع المسيح 7
The Holy Spirit الروح القدس 17
The Cross الصليب 20
Why The Cross? لماذا الصليب 29
The Bible الكتاب المقدس 33
The Infallibility Of The Bible عصمة الكتاب المقدس 39
Love المحبة 44
Forgiveness الغفران 50
Paradise الجنّة 54
Women النساء 58
The Excellency Of The Bible معجزة الكتاب المقدس 62

FOREWORD

"The Truth of the Quran in the Light of the Bible" is designed to be a study book. Verses are given from both the Quran and the Bible to demonstrate the points made, but these are only examples, and the reader is encouraged to seek out others. This book is written for followers both of the Bible and of the Quran, with the hope of providing each with a better understanding of the truth.

The Quran is often spelled Koran, but the former spelling is more accurate. Quranic verses have been provided in Arabic as well as English, since the Quran is written in the Arabic language.

The Quran contains 114 books, called suras. The suras are not divided into chapters as in the Bible. The first number in each reference corresponds with the name of that sura; the following numbers are the verses. For example, Al-Nur 24:35 is Sura Al-Nur, verse 35, 24 is the number of this sura, making it easier to locate in the Quran.

The Bible has 66 books. Biblical references are given as the name of the book first, then the chapter number, followed by the verses within that chapter. For example, John 8:12 is the Gospel According to the Apostle John, chapter 8, verse 12. 1 John 1:9 is the First Letter of the Apostle John, chapter 1, verse 9. Biblical verses are taken from the King James version, and the reader is invited to study these references in other versions as well (such as the New King James version) which combine accurate translation with modern vocabulary.

This book was first compiled in 1976 in England. The third edition (1985) was revised to include the Arabic text for the Quranic verses. This is now the eighth edition, and it is our prayer that God will use these words, as the Apostle Paul prayed, "that your love may abound yet more and more in knowledge and in all judgment; that ye may approve things that are excellent" (Philippians 1:9-10).

Rev. Victor Khalil, Th.D.
January 2009

INTRODUCTION

For those who seek the truth it is not hard to find, if sought sincerely, unselfishly, and with the aim that not only they but others might be benefited by it. If scientists were to keep their discoveries to themselves, what a poor world this would be! If Thomas Edison had not shared his discovery of electrical current with us, we would still be living by gaslight. Similarly, where would we be without the aid of machines and modern technology?

Just as we appreciate the light given by electricity, we should appreciate the spiritual light present in the One who says, "I am the Light of the world" (John 8:12). The Islamic scriptures, the Quran, also speak of the light to mankind: "Allah is the Light of the heavens and of the earth" (Al-Nur 24:35).

اللَّهُ نُورُ السَّمَوَاتِ وَالْأَرْضِ. سورة النور 35

It should be more than a matter of appreciation, but one of deep gratitude, that our God has chosen to lead us by His Word through this world of sin and confusion where man has strayed away from his Creator.

That man needs divine help can be seen in both the Bible and the Quran, respectively: "Teach me thy way, O Lord, and lead me in a plain path" (Psalms 27:11). "And see if there be any wicked way in me and lead me in the way everlasting" (Psalms 139:24). "Guide us along the straight path" (Al-Fatiha 1:6).

اهْدِنَا الصِّرَاطَ الْمُسْتَقِيمَ. سورة الفاتحة 6

If the Word of God is to be man's guide, it must be pursued and studied so that man can know in whom he puts his trust. Regardless of whether one believes in the Bible or the Quran as the "descended" Word of God, it is essential to approach either book with an open mind, free from any preconceived or inherited ideas. The only way to be honest with oneself is to accept the truth as revealed by God.

The approach of this book is not meant to be critical. Its aim is to focus the reader's mind on God's Word and to reveal the many blessings obtainable through it, which might otherwise be overlooked. We will focus on the religious books of two major religions: the Bible of Christianity, and the Quran of Islam. However, we must consider the fact that the Bible does not concern only the Christian. In fact, more than two thirds of it concerns the Jews. So if Christians had at any time thought of altering their Bible, it would have been with great antagonism from the Jews, and one can only imagine the endless problems! Therefore, the allegation that the Bible has been altered is illogical. This subject will be discussed in some detail later.

I pray that as you read this book that Allah, the Almighty, may open your eyes to see the true Light that has come into our world. May the Light enter into your heart and the hearts of many.

GOD: ALLAH الله

Christians and Muslims meet at this very high point—both believe in God. Likewise, many of His attributes will be equally praised by both.

Allah, the Almighty	الله سبحانه وتعالى
He is holy: "Quddus"	قدوس
He is able: "Qadir"	قادر
He is living: "Heyy"	حي
. . . and so on.	

Allah in the Quranic Scriptures

He is omnipotent: "Al-Maqtadir"   المقتدر
"So we seized them, with the seizure of One Mighty, Omnipotent" (Al-Qamar 54:42).

فَأَخَذْنَاهُمْ أَخْذَ عَزِيزٍ مُقْتَدِرٍ. سورة القمر 42

He is omniscient: "Al-Aleem" العليم
"Allah is indeed all-knowing" (Al-Hajj 22:59)

وَإِنَّ اللَّهَ لَعَلِيمٌ حَلِيمٌ. سورة الحج 59

He is all seeing: "Al-Baseer" البصير
He is all-hearing: "Al-Samea" السميع
"Allah is all-hearing, all-seeing" (Al-Nisa 4:58).

إِنَّ اللَّهَ كَانَ سَمِيعًا بَصِيرًا. سورة النساء 58

He is the Creator: "Al-Khaliq" الخالق
"Has not He who created the heavens and the earth the power to create the like of them? Yea, and He is indeed the Supreme Creator, the all-knowing" (Ya-Sin 36:81)

أَوَلَيْسَ الَّذِي خَلَقَ السَّمَوَاتِ وَالْأَرْضَ بِقَادِرٍ عَلَى أَنْ يَخْلُقَ مِثْلَهُمْ بَلَى وَهُوَ الْخَلَّاقُ الْعَلِيمُ. سورة يس 81

He is living: "Al-Heyy" الحي
"Allah…the ever-living" (Al-Baqarah 2:255).

اللَّهُ لَا إِلَهَ إِلَّا هُوَ الْحَيُّ الْقَيُّومُ. سورة البقرة 255

He is One (single): "Al-Wahid" الواحد
"Proclaim: He is Allah, the Single; Allah, the Self-Existing and besought of all. He begets not, nor is He begotten; and there is no one like unto Him" (Al-Ikhlas 112:1-4).

قُلْ هُوَ اللَّهُ أَحَدٌ (1) اللَّهُ الصَّمَدُ (2) لَمْ يَلِدْ وَلَمْ يُولَدْ (3) وَلَمْ يَكُنْ لَهُ كُفُوًا أَحَدٌ (4). سورة الإخلاص 1-4

God in the Biblical Scriptures

"Behold, God is mighty, and despiseth not any; He is mighty in strength and wisdom" (Job 36:5).

"Now we are sure that Thou knowest all things" (John 16:30).

"The eyes of the Lord are in every place, beholding the evil and the good" (Proverbs 15:3).

"Thou art worthy, O Lord,…for Thou hast created all things" (Revelation 4:11).

"For I know that my Redeemer liveth" (Job 19:25).

"See now that I, even I, am He, and there is no god with me" (Deuteronomy 32:39).

These are just a few of the many verses describing attributes of God in each book.

Understanding the Christian Doctrine of God

A few points of clarification may be helpful. Some "Christian" heretics who lived at the time of Muhammad believed in the existence of more than one God. Their "Trinity" consisted of "Allah" الله(God), "Saheba" صاحبة(Mary, the wife of God), and "Isa" عيسى (Jesus, her son). There is no verse in the whole Bible that supports this false doctrine.

The idiom "Son" that Christians use is the same as the idiom "Word" which describes Jesus Christ in the Quran: "Call to mind when the angel said to Mary: Allah, through His Word, gives thee glad tidings of a son named the Messiah, Jesus, son of Mary, honored in this world and the next, and of those who are granted nearness to Allah" (Al-Imran 3:45).

إِذْ قَالَتِ الْمَلَائِكَةُ يَا مَرْيَمُ إِنَّ اللَّهَ يُبَشِّرُكِ بِكَلِمَةٍ مِنْهُ اسْمُهُ الْمَسِيحُ عِيسَى ابْنُ مَرْيَمَ وَجِيهًا فِي الدُّنْيَا وَالْآخِرَةِ وَمِنَ الْمُقَرَّبِينَ . سورة آل عمران 45

And in the Bible: "In the beginning was the Word and the Word was with God, and the Word was God…And the Word was made flesh, and dwelt among us" (John 1:1,14).

God Revealed to Man

Both Muslims and Christians agree that God, the Almighty, is omnipotent. The Quran also called God "The Manifest"—"Al-Zahir." الظاهر "He is the First and the Last and the Manifest and the Hidden, and He has full knowledge of all things" (Al-Hadid 57:3).

هُوَ الأول وَالْآخِرُ وَالظَّاهِرُ وَالْبَاطِنُ وَهُوَ بِكُلِّ شَيْءٍ عَلِيم . سورة الحديد 3

He reveals Himself in various ways: "It is not given to a man that Allah should speak to him except by revelation or from behind a veil or by sending a messenger to reveal by His command that which He pleases. Thus have we revealed to thee a Spirit by our command" (Al-Shura 42:51-52).

(51)وَمَا كَانَ لِبَشَرٍ أَنْ يُكَلِّمَهُ اللَّهُ إِلَّا وَحْيًا أَوْ مِنْ وَرَاءِ حِجَابٍ أَوْ يُرْسِلَ رَسُولًا فَيُوحِيَ بِإِذْنِهِ مَا يَشَاءُ إِنَّهُ عَلِيٌّ حَكِيمٌ (51) وَكَذَلِكَ أَوْحَيْنَا إِلَيْكَ رُوحًا مِنْ أَمْرِنَا مَا كُنْتَ تَدْرِي مَا الْكِتَابُ وَلَا الْإِيمَانُ وَلَكِنْ جَعَلْنَاهُ نُورًا نَهْدِي بِهِ مَنْ نَشَاءُ مِنْ عِبَادِنَا وَإِنَّكَ لَتَهْدِي إِلَى صِرَاطٍ مُسْتَقِيمٍ . سورة الشورى 51-52

He reveals Himself through His chosen servants: "Indeed, Allah has conferred a great favor on the believers by raising among them a Messenger from among themselves, who recites to them His Signs, and purifies them and teaches them the Book and

Wisdom. Before that, they were surely in manifest error" (Al-Imran 3:164).

لَقَدْ مَنَّ اللَّهُ عَلَى الْمُؤْمِنِينَ إِذْ بَعَثَ فِيهِمْ رَسُولًا مِنْ أَنْفُسِهِمْ يَتْلُو عَلَيْهِمْ آيَاتِهِ وَيُزَكِّيهِمْ وَيُعَلِّمُهُمُ الْكِتَابَ وَالْحِكْمَةَ وَإِنْ كَانُوا مِنْ قَبْلُ لَفِي ضَلَالٍ مُبِينٍ .

سورة آل عمران 164

Similarly, the Bible illustrates this: "God, who at sundry times and in diverse manners spake in time past unto the fathers by the prophets..." (Hebrews 1:1).

"Surely the Lord God will do nothing, but He revealeth His secret unto His servants, the prophets" (Amos 3:7).

"For therein is the righteousness of God revealed from faith to faith: as it is written, the just shall live by faith" (Romans 1:17).

Who is Allah?

Do Christians, Jews, and Muslims worship the same God? Confusion has arisen from the use of the name "Allah" for god in the Quran, and the Arabic translation of the name for God as "Allah" in the Christian Bible. This topic is very complex and elaborate, and as always, I encourage all to research further if needed.

Most of my knowledge comes from being raised in a Muslim country and educated in Muslim schools. In addition, my passion to understand and expose God's truth has compelled me to thoroughly research the topic over my lifetime.

To clarify, Allah was known to the Arabs in Saudi Arabia before Islam existed, although originally known as Al-Lat. This god was identified as a moon god and was one of the 360 gods worshipped by the tribes in Mecca. Al-Lat was one of the main gods of the Quarish tribe that was located in Mecca. Muhammad was from this tribe, and when conceiving the religion of Islam, designated this god as the supreme god of Islam.

In order to maintain peace among his tribe when branching off into Islam, he adopted another of their gods, "the black stone". This stone is now an important part of Islam as many travel to Mecca once a year to honor it. About 227 years after the death of Muhammad, Muslim scholars changed the name of the god of Islam from Al-Lat to Allah.

Allah in Arabic became the word for "god." Years later, when the Bible was translated into Arabic, the translators used the name Allah for the God of the Bible because the name was already commonly known to the Arabs as God. It was not meant to be confused with the god of Islam. Today, many Arabic-speaking Christian scholars and converts (Muslims who have become Christians) are using Hebrew names for God from the Bible such as Arrab Al-Elah, which means "the Lord God," Elohim and/or Yahweh to prevent further confusion.

The concept of "Allah" in Islam is different from "Allah" in the Bible. Although there are many differentiations, the most obvious is that Allah in Islam is a distant, non-relational god that is feared in a negative manner. Allah has 99 names in the Quran, however, the name "God is love" is not found as it is in the Christian Bible. The God of the Bible is loving and merciful, yet holy and just, deserving of our respect. His main desire is that all love Him and one another with a pure love.

ISA: JESUS CHRIST عيسى - يسوع المسيح

The Quran calls Jesus "Isa," "Christ, the son of Mary," and "the Messiah." "Indeed, Christ, Isa, the son of Mary is a Messenger ("Apostle") of Allah and His word conveyed to Mary and a Spirit from Him" (Al-Nisa 4:171).

يَا أَهْلَ الْكِتَابِ لَا تَغْلُوا فِي دِينِكُمْ وَلَا تَقُولُوا عَلَى اللَّهِ إِلَّا الْحَقَّ إِنَّمَا الْمَسِيحُ عِيسَى ابْنُ مَرْيَمَ رَسُولُ اللَّهِ وَكَلِمَتُهُ أَلْقَاهَا إِلَى مَرْيَمَ وَرُوحٌ مِنْهُ فَآمِنُوا بِاللَّهِ وَرُسُلِهِ وَلَا تَقُولُوا ثَلَاثَةٌ انْتَهُوا خَيْرًا لَكُمْ إِنَّمَا اللَّهُ إِلَهٌ وَاحِدٌ سُبْحَانَهُ أَنْ يَكُونَ لَهُ وَلَدٌ لَهُ مَا فِي السَّمَوَاتِ وَمَا فِي الْأَرْضِ وَكَفَى بِاللَّهِ وَكِيلًا . النساء 171

Christ's position in the Quran is described as one of reputation and acclaim. Not even a prophet, nor Muhammad himself, receives such exaltation in the Quran as Christ does. We find in the Quran that Muhammad needed his sins to be forgiven: "Allah has turned with 'taba' تاب (forgiveness) to the Prophet (Muhammad) and to the Emigrants and the Helpers who stood by him in the hour of distress when the hearts of a party of them had wellnigh swerved, and He (Allah) has turned with forgiveness to them" (Al-Tauba 9:117).

لَقَدْ تَابَ اللَّهُ عَلَى النَّبِيِّ وَالْمُهَاجِرِينَ وَالْأَنْصَارِ الَّذِينَ اتَّبَعُوهُ فِي سَاعَةِ الْعُسْرَةِ مِنْ بَعْدِ مَا كَادَ يَزِيغُ قُلُوبُ فَرِيقٍ مِنْهُمْ ثُمَّ تَابَ عَلَيْهِمْ إِنَّهُ بِهِمْ رَءُوفٌ رَحِيمٌ . التوبة 117

Jesus Exalted in the Quran

The following are a few examples of Jesus Christ being exalted:

1. <u>Born of a Virgin</u>: "The angel said to Mary: I am but a messenger from thy Lord that I may give thee tidings of a righteous son who will grow up to maturity. She marveled: How shall it be that I shall have a grown son, seeing that no man has touched me and I have not been unchaste? The angel said: So it is, but the Lord sayeth: It is easy for me" (Maryam 19:19-20).

(18) قَالَ إِنَّمَا أَنَا رَسُولُ رَبِّكِ لِأَهَبَ لَكِ غُلَامًا زَكِيًّا (19) قَالَتْ أَنَّى يَكُونُ لِي غُلَامٌ وَلَمْ يَمْسَسْنِي بَشَرٌ وَلَمْ أَكُ بَغِيًّا (20) قَالَ كَذَلِكِ قَالَ رَبُّكِ هُوَ عَلَيَّ هَيِّنٌ وَلِنَجْعَلَهُ آيَةً لِلنَّاسِ وَرَحْمَةً مِنَّا وَكَانَ أَمْرًا مَقْضِيًّا . سورة مريم 19-20

"Call to mind when the angels said to Mary: Allah, through His word, gives thee glad tidings of a son named the Messiah, Jesus son of Mary, honored in this world and the next, and of those who are granted nearness to Allah. He shall admonish people in his early years and also in his ripe years, and he shall be of the righteous…He (Allah) will teach him the Book and the Wisdom and the Torah and the Gospel and will make him a Messenger to the children of Israel, bearing the message: I have come to you with a Sign from your Lord that for your benefit, in the manner of a bird, I shall fashion…" (Al-Imran 3:45-50).

إِذْ قَالَتِ الْمَلَائِكَةُ يَا مَرْيَمُ إِنَّ اللَّهَ يُبَشِّرُكِ بِكَلِمَةٍ مِنْهُ اسْمُهُ الْمَسِيحُ عِيسَى ابْنُ مَرْيَمَ وَجِيهًا فِي الدُّنْيَا وَالْآخِرَةِ وَمِنَ الْمُقَرَّبِينَ (45) وَيُكَلِّمُ النَّاسَ فِي الْمَهْدِ وَكَهْلًا وَمِنَ الصَّالِحِينَ (46) قَالَتْ رَبِّ أَنَّى يَكُونُ لِي وَلَدٌ وَلَمْ يَمْسَسْنِي بَشَرٌ قَالَ كَذَلِكِ اللَّهُ يَخْلُقُ مَا يَشَاءُ إِذَا قَضَى أَمْرًا فَإِنَّمَا يَقُولُ لَهُ كُنْ فَيَكُونُ (47) وَيُعَلِّمُهُ الْكِتَابَ وَالْحِكْمَةَ وَالتَّوْرَاةَ وَالْإِنْجِيلَ (48) وَرَسُولًا إِلَى بَنِي إِسْرَائِيلَ أَنِّي قَدْ جِئْتُكُمْ بِآيَةٍ مِنْ رَبِّكُمْ أَنِّي أَخْلُقُ لَكُمْ مِنَ الطِّينِ كَهَيْئَةِ الطَّيْرِ فَأَنْفُخُ فِيهِ فَيَكُونُ طَيْرًا بِإِذْنِ اللَّهِ وَأُبْرِئُ الْأَكْمَهَ وَالْأَبْرَصَ وَأُحْيِي الْمَوْتَى بِإِذْنِ اللَّهِ وَأُنَبِّئُكُمْ بِمَا تَأْكُلُونَ وَمَا تَدَّخِرُونَ فِي بُيُوتِكُمْ إِنَّ فِي ذَلِكَ لَآيَةً لَكُمْ إِنْ كُنْتُمْ مُؤْمِنِينَ (49) وَمُصَدِّقًا لِمَا بَيْنَ يَدَيَّ مِنَ التَّوْرَاةِ وَلِأُحِلَّ لَكُمْ بَعْضَ الَّذِي حُرِّمَ عَلَيْكُمْ وَجِئْتُكُمْ بِآيَةٍ مِنْ رَبِّكُمْ فَاتَّقُوا اللَّهَ وَأَطِيعُونِ (50) إِنَّ اللَّهَ رَبِّي وَرَبُّكُمْ فَاعْبُدُوهُ هَذَا صِرَاطٌ مُسْتَقِيمٌ .
سورة آل عمران 45-50

2. <u>Born of the Holy Spirit</u>: "We have breathed our Spirit into her (Mary), and we have made her and her son a Sign for peoples" (Al-Anbiya 21:91).

وَالَّتِي أَحْصَنَتْ فَرْجَهَا فَنَفَخْنَا فِيهَا مِنْ رُوحِنَا وَجَعَلْنَاهَا وَابْنَهَا آيَةً لِلْعَالَمِينَ .
الأنبياء 19

3. <u>Spoke at His birth</u>: People said to Mary, "How can we hold converse with one whom was but yesterday a child being rocked in a cradle? Jesus taught: I am a servant of Allah, He has appointed me a prophet. He has made me blessed wheresoever I may be" (Maryam 19:29-31).

فَأَشَارَتْ إِلَيْهِ قَالُوا كَيْفَ نُكَلِّمُ مَنْ كَانَ فِي الْمَهْدِ صَبِيًّا (29) قَالَ إِنِّي عَبْدُ اللَّهِ وَأَوْصَانِي بِالصَّلَاةِ آتَانِيَ وَجَعَلَنِي نَبِيًّا (30) وَجَعَلَنِي مُبَارَكًا أَيْنَ مَا كُنْتُ وَالزَّكَاةِ مَا دُمْتُ حَيًّا. مريم 29-31

4. <u>Strengthened by the Holy Spirit</u>: "We gave Jesus, son of Mary, clear proofs and strengthened him with the Spirit of holiness" (Al-Baraqah 2:253).

تِلْكَ الرُّسُلُ فَضَّلْنَا بَعْضَهُمْ عَلَى بَعْضٍ مِنْهُمْ مَنْ كَلَّمَ اللَّهُ وَرَفَعَ بَعْضَهُمْ دَرَجَاتٍ وَآتَيْنَا عِيسَى ابْنَ مَرْيَمَ الْبَيِّنَاتِ وَأَيَّدْنَاهُ بِرُوحِ الْقُدُسِ وَلَوْ شَاءَ اللَّهُ مَا اقْتَتَلَ الَّذِينَ

مِنْ بَعْدِهِمْ مِنْ بَعْدِ مَا جَاءَتْهُمُ الْبَيِّنَاتُ وَلَكِنِ اخْتَلَفُوا فَمِنْهُمْ مَنْ آمَنَ وَمِنْهُمْ مَنْ كَفَرَ وَلَوْ شَاءَ اللَّهُ مَا اقْتَتَلُوا وَلَكِنَّ اللَّهَ يَفْعَلُ مَا يُرِيدُ . البقرة 253

5. <u>He is blessed</u>: "Jesus taught:…He (Allah) has made me blessed wheresoever I may be" (Maryam 19:31).

وَأَوْصَانِي بِالصَّلَاةِ وَالزَّكَاةِ مَا دُمْتُ حَيًّا مريم وَجَعَلَنِي مُبَارَكًا أَيْنَ مَا كُنْتُ . مريم 31

6. <u>He is the fulfillment of the Old Testament prophecies</u>: "I fulfill that which has been sent down before me, namely the Torah. And I shall make lawful for you some of that which was forbidden you. I come to you with a Sign from your Lord; so be mindful of your duty to Allah and obey" (Al-Imran 3:50).

وَمُصَدِّقًا لِمَا بَيْنَ يَدَيَّ مِنَ التَّوْرَاةِ وَلِأُحِلَّ لَكُمْ بَعْضَ الَّذِي حُرِّمَ عَلَيْكُمْ وَجِئْتُكُمْ بِآيَةٍ مِنْ رَبِّكُمْ فَاتَّقُوا اللَّهَ وَأَطِيعُونِ . آل عمران 50

7. <u>He is the Word of God</u>: "Jesus, son of Mary, was but a Messenger of Allah and His word conveyed to Mary and a Spirit from Him" (Al-Nisa 4:171).

يَا أَهْلَ الْكِتَابِ لَا تَغْلُوا فِي دِينِكُمْ وَلَا تَقُولُوا عَلَى اللَّهِ إِلَّا الْحَقَّ إِنَّمَا الْمَسِيحُ عِيسَى ابْنُ مَرْيَمَ رَسُولُ اللَّهِ وَكَلِمَتُهُ أَلْقَاهَا إِلَى مَرْيَمَ وَرُوحٌ مِنْهُ فَآمِنُوا بِاللَّهِ وَرُسُلِهِ وَلَا تَقُولُوا ثَلَاثَةٌ انْتَهُوا خَيْرًا لَكُمْ إِنَّمَا اللَّهُ إِلَهٌ وَاحِدٌ سُبْحَانَهُ أَنْ يَكُونَ لَهُ وَلَدٌ لَهُ مَا فِي السَّمَوَاتِ وَمَا فِي الْأَرْضِ وَكَفَى بِاللَّهِ وَكِيلًا . النساء 171

8. <u>He is alive</u>: "Allah ascended him to Himself" (Al-Nisa 4:158).

بَلْ رَفَعَهُ اللَّهُ إِلَيْهِ وَكَانَ اللَّهُ عَزِيزًا حَكِيمًا . النساء 158

"Allah said: O Isa, I shall cause thee to die, and causing thee to ascend to Me, and am cleansing thee of those who disbelieve" (Al-Imran 3:55).

إِذْ قَالَ اللَّهُ يَا عِيسَى إِنِّي مُتَوَفِّيكَ وَرَافِعُكَ إِلَيَّ وَمُطَهِّرُكَ مِنَ الَّذِينَ كَفَرُوا وَجَاعِلُ الَّذِينَ اتَّبَعُوكَ فَوْقَ الَّذِينَ كَفَرُوا إِلَى يَوْمِ الْقِيَامَةِ ثُمَّ إِلَيَّ مَرْجِعُكُمْ فَأَحْكُمُ بَيْنَكُمْ فِيمَا كُنْتُمْ فِيهِ تَخْتَلِفُونَ . آل عمران 55

9. <u>He is Lord</u>: "They have taken their divines and their monks for lords rather than Allah and Christ, the son of Mary" (Al-Tauba 9:31).

اتَّخَذُوا أَحْبَارَهُمْ وَرُهْبَانَهُمْ أَرْبَابًا مِنْ دُونِ اللَّهِ وَالْمَسِيحَ ابْنَ مَرْيَمَ وَمَا أُمِرُوا إِلَّا لِيَعْبُدُوا إِلَهًا وَاحِدًا لَا إِلَهَ إِلَّا هُوَ سُبْحَانَهُ عَمَّا يُشْرِكُونَ . التوبة 31

10. <u>He is Creator</u>: "And (make Him) an apostle to the children of Israel: that I (Jesus) have come to you with a sign from your Lord. That I create for you out of dust like the form of a bird, then I breathe into it and it becomes a bird with Allah's permission" (Al-Imran 3:49).

وَرَسُولًا إِلَى بَنِي إِسْرَائِيلَ أَنِّي قَدْ جِئْتُكُمْ بِآيَةٍ مِنْ رَبِّكُمْ أَنِّي أَخْلُقُ لَكُمْ مِنَ الطِّينِ كَهَيْئَةِ الطَّيْرِ فَأَنْفُخُ فِيهِ فَيَكُونُ طَيْرًا بِإِذْنِ اللَّهِ وَأُبْرِئُ الْأَكْمَهَ وَالْأَبْرَصَ وَأُحْيِي الْمَوْتَى بِإِذْنِ اللَّهِ وَأُنَبِّئُكُمْ بِمَا تَأْكُلُونَ وَمَا تَدَّخِرُونَ فِي بُيُوتِكُمْ إِنَّ فِي ذَلِكَ لَآيَةً لَكُمْ إِنْ كُنْتُمْ مُؤْمِنِينَ . آل عمران 49

11. <u>His followers are exalted</u>: "Allah said: O Jesus! I will…make those who follow you above those who disbelieve to the day of resurrection" (Al-Imran 3:55).

إِذْ قَالَ اللَّهُ يَا عِيسَى إِنِّي مُتَوَفِّيكَ وَرَافِعُكَ إِلَيَّ وَمُطَهِّرُكَ مِنَ الَّذِينَ كَفَرُوا وَجَاعِلُ الَّذِينَ اتَّبَعُوكَ فَوْقَ الَّذِينَ كَفَرُوا إِلَى يَوْمِ الْقِيَامَةِ ثُمَّ إِلَيَّ مَرْجِعُكُمْ فَأَحْكُمُ بَيْنَكُمْ فِيمَا كُنْتُمْ فِيهِ تَخْتَلِفُونَ . آل عمران 55

12. <u>He is the advocate</u>: The Sura (book) of Zumar limits the position of advocate to God. "Say: Allah's is the intercession altogether" (Al-Zumar 39:44).

قُلْ لِلَّهِ الشَّفَاعَةُ جَمِيعًا لَهُ مُلْكُ السَّمَاوَاتِ وَالْأَرْضِ ثُمَّ إِلَيْهِ تُرْجَعُونَ . الزمر 44

However, we find that Jesus Christ is an intercessor in heaven. "When the angels said, 'O Mary! Surely Allah gives you good news with a word from Him whose name is Christ, Isa, son of Mary, honored in this world and the hereafter, and of those who are made near (to Allah)<?>...'" (Al-Imran 3:45)[1].

إِذْ قَالَتِ الْمَلَائِكَةُ يَا مَرْيَمُ إِنَّ اللَّهَ يُبَشِّرُكِ بِكَلِمَةٍ مِنْهُ اسْمُهُ الْمَسِيحُ عِيسَى ابْنُ مَرْيَمَ وَجِيهًا فِي الدُّنْيَا وَالْآخِرَةِ وَمِنَ الْمُقَرَّبِينَ. آل عمران 45

This implies that He is an advocate, as Al Galalan's[2] paraphrase to this verse says Jesus is "honored (wajeh) on earth by prophecy and in the life after was made near to God by intercession." Al Razy[2] says that "honored" (wajeh) means that God answered His prayers on earth and He was able to raise the dead. At the end of the world He will make Jesus one of those near to Him by making him an advocate for His people.

13. <u>He performed miracles</u>: "Jesus said...I shall declare clean the blind and the leprous and shall bestow life on the spiritually dead by the command of Allah" (Al-Imran 3:49).

وَرَسُولًا إِلَى بَنِي إِسْرَائِيلَ أَنِّي قَدْ جِئْتُكُمْ بِآيَةٍ مِنْ رَبِّكُمْ أَنِّي أَخْلُقُ لَكُمْ مِنَ الطِّينِ كَهَيْئَةِ الطَّيْرِ فَأَنْفُخُ فِيهِ فَيَكُونُ طَيْرًا بِإِذْنِ اللَّهِ وَأُبْرِئُ الْأَكْمَهَ وَالْأَبْرَصَ وَأُحْيِي الْمَوْتَى بِإِذْنِ اللَّهِ وَأُنَبِّئُكُمْ بِمَا تَأْكُلُونَ وَمَا تَدَّخِرُونَ فِي بُيُوتِكُمْ إِنَّ فِي ذَلِكَ لَآيَةً لَكُمْ إِنْ كُنْتُمْ مُؤْمِنِينَ . آل عمران 49

---

[1] Literal translation
[2] Muslim scholars

Jesus in the Bible

In the same way and more, we find Jesus Christ exalted and honored in the Bible. The following are some of the many verses from the Bible:

1. <u>Born of a virgin</u>: "Therefore the Lord Himself shall give you a sign, Behold, a virgin shall conceive, and bear a son and shall call His name Immanuel." (Isaiah 7:14). This prophecy was fulfilled in the New Testament, when the angel said to Mary, "'And behold, thou shalt conceive in thy womb, and bring forth a son, and shall call His name Jesus.'....Then said Mary unto the angel, 'How shall this be, seeing I know not a man?'" (Luke 1:31-32).

2. <u>Born of the Holy Spirit</u>: "And the angel answered and said unto her, (Mary) 'the Holy Ghost shall come upon thee, and the power of the Highest shall overshadow thee'" (Luke 1:35).

3. <u>Strengthened by the Holy Spirit</u>: "The Spirit of the Lord God is upon me (Jesus) because the Lord hath anointed me to preach good tidings unto the meek" (Isaiah 61:1). The fulfillment in the New Testament: "And Jesus, when He was baptized, went up straightway out of the water: and, lo, the heavens were opened unto Him, and He saw the Spirit of God descending like a dove and lighting upon Him..." (Matthew 3:16).

4. <u>He is blessed</u>: "And Elisabeth was filled with the Holy Ghost and she spake out with a loud voice, and said (to Mary), 'Blessed art thou among women, and blessed is the fruit of thy womb'" (Luke 1:41-42).

5. <u>He performed miracles</u>: "And Jesus went about all Galilee, teaching in their synagogues, and preaching the Gospel of the Kingdom, and healing all manner of sickness and all manner of disease among the people" (Matthew 4:23).

6. <u>He is the fulfillment of the Old Testament prophecies</u>: "God who at sundry times and divers manners spake in time past unto the fathers by prophets has in these last days spoken unto us by His Son" (Hebrews 1:1-2).

7. <u>He is the Word of God</u>: "In the beginning was the Word and the Word was with God, and the Word was God" (John 1:1).

8. <u>He is alive</u>: "I am He that liveth, and was dead; and behold, I am alive forevermore" (Revelation 1:18).

9. <u>He is Lord</u>: "…God hath made that same Jesus, whom ye have crucified, both Lord and Christ" (Acts 2:36).

10. <u>He is the Creator</u>: "All things were made by Him; and without Him was not anything made that was made" (John 1:3).

11. <u>His followers are exalted</u>: "And Jesus said unto them (His disciples), 'Verily I say unto you, that ye which have followed me, in the regeneration when the Son of man shall sit in the throne of His glory, ye also shall sit upon twelve thrones, judging the twelve tribes of Israel'" (Matthew 19:28).

12. <u>He is the advocate</u>: "…We have an advocate with the Father, Jesus Christ the righteous" (1 John 2:1).

13. <u>He is impeccable, sinless</u>: "Jesus said, 'Which of you convinceth me of sin?'" (John 8:46).

The word "Son" used by Christians for Jesus does not imply fleshly sonship. Christians do not believe that "Allah" was married or had a wife. Some Muslims perhaps misunderstand the meaning of the word "Son" as mentioned in the Bible. It is the same meaning as the title "Word" which is used in the Quran.

The Quran confirms the sincerity of Jesus' message and that He is impeccable, which means that He does not lie, and that whatever He says about Himself is true and must be regarded as important to our lives. In this case, the following Scriptures, and others like them, must be accepted as true. Jesus said:

14. "I am the light of the world: he that followeth me shall not walk in darkness, but shall have the light of life" (John 8:12).

15. "I am the way, the truth, and the life: no man cometh unto the Father, but by me" (John 14:6).

16. "I am the bread of life: he that cometh to me shall never hunger; and he that believeth on me shall never thirst" (John 6:35).

17. "I am the resurrection, and the life: he that believeth in me, though he were dead, yet shall he live" (John 11:25).

Muslims as well as Christians believe that Mary was chosen by Allah for the birth of Jesus Christ. "And when the angels said: O Mary! Surely Allah has chosen you and purified you and chosen you above the women of the world" (Al-Amran 3:42).

وَإِذْ قَالَتِ الْمَلَائِكَةُ يَا مَرْيَمُ إِنَّ اللَّهَ اصْطَفَاكِ وَطَهَّرَكِ وَاصْطَفَاكِ عَلَى نِسَاءِ الْعَالَمِينَ

آل عمران 42

"And the angel said to her, 'Fear not, Mary: for thou hast found favor with God'" (Luke 1:30).

Mary, herself, drew people's attention to her son and commanded the servants at the wedding in Cana of Galilee to listen to Him. "His mother saith unto the servants, 'Whatsoever He saith unto you, do it'" (John 2:5).

This includes everyone today, too, for what Jesus said then applies to us today. So, let us listen to Him who tells the truth, and believe what He says.

THE HOLY SPIRIT الروح القدس

The Holy Spirit is mentioned in the Quran as the strengthener and the sustainer of Jesus Christ: "And we gave Jesus, the son of Mary, manifest signs and strengthened Him with the Holy Spirit" (Al-Baqarah 2:87).

وَلَقَدْ آتَيْنَا مُوسَى الْكِتَابَ وَقَفَّيْنَا مِنْ بَعْدِهِ بِالرُّسُلِ وَآتَيْنَا عِيسَى ابْنَ مَرْيَمَ الْبَيِّنَاتِ وَأَيَّدْنَاهُ بِرُوحِ الْقُدُسِ أَفَكُلَّمَا جَاءَكُمْ رَسُولٌ بِمَا لا تَهْوَى أَنْفُسُكُمُ اسْتَكْبَرْتُمْ فَفَرِيقًا كَذَّبْتُمْ وَفَرِيقًا تَقْتُلُونَ . البقرة 87

A teaching has arisen among some Muslims that the original word for Holy Spirit ("Paraclete" in Greek) should be translated "Muhammad" and that the Christians have translated it as "Comforter" or "Holy Spirit" to suit their beliefs. They claim that Jesus Christ spoke of Muhammad, the "Paraclete," when He spoke of "One to follow after" Him, but they forget to continue on with what Jesus said about that "Paraclete" and his characteristics. Jesus said, "For if I go not away, the Comforter will not come unto you; but if I depart, I will send Him unto you" (John 16:7). The promise was for the disciples, and was for an immediate

Comforter to replace Jesus. If Muhammad was the Comforter or "Paraclete", it means that the disciples themselves were left without a Comforter since Muhammad's message began more than 600 years after Christ.

Who Is the Paraclete?

The characteristics of the Comforter described by Jesus clearly distinguish him as the Holy Spirit:

1. "And I will pray the Father, and He shall give you another Comforter, that He may abide with you forever" (John 14:16). Muhammad is dead, but the Comforter will abide forever.

2. "…Even the Spirit of truth (Comforter) whom the world cannot receive, because it seeth Him not, neither knoweth Him; but ye know Him; for He dwelleth with you, and shall be in you" (John 14:17).

3. "But when the Comforter is come, whom I will send unto you from the Father, even the Spirit of truth, which proceedeth from the Father, He shall testify of me" (John 15:26). If this were the case, Muhammad should have testified of Christ.

4. "And when He (the Comforter) is come, He will reprove the world of sin, and of righteousness, and of judgment: Of sin because they believe not in me…" (John 16:8-9). Muhammad should have condemned the world of unbelief in Christ.

5. "Howbeit, when He, the Spirit of truth is come He will guide you into all truth, for He shall not speak of Himself; but

whatsoever He shall hear, that shall He speak: and He will show you things to come. He shall glorify me: for He shall receive of mine, and shall show it unto you" (John 16:13-14). Muhammad, if he had been the Paraclete, should have been guiding people to Christ, speaking of Christ, listening to Christ, glorifying and teaching of Jesus.

NONE OF THE ABOVE VERSES ABOUT THE "PARACLETE," THE COMFORTER, AND THE HOLY SPIRIT IS APPLICABLE TO MUHAMMAD.

THE CROSS الصليب

"It is a stumbling block."

This is how the Muslims and many nominal Christians see it. We are not surprised to hear the Apostle Paul, a follower of Jesus and His cross, saying the same thing: "But we preach Christ crucified, unto the Jews a stumbling block, and unto the Greeks foolishness" (1 Corinthians 1:23).

The Quran teaches that Christ was not crucified but God has 'ascended' Him to heaven. "And this saying: surely we have killed Christ, Isa the son of Mary, the apostle of Allah: and they did not kill Him nor did they crucify Him but was made dubious to then, and those who differ therein are only in a doubt about it… but Allah has ascended Him to Himself: and Allah is Mighty, Wise" (Al-Nisa 4:157-158).

وَقَوْلِهِمْ إِنَّا قَتَلْنَا الْمَسِيحَ عِيسَى ابْنَ مَرْيَمَ رَسُولَ اللَّهِ وَمَا قَتَلُوهُ وَمَا صَلَبُوهُ وَلَٰكِنْ شُبِّهَ لَهُمْ وَإِنَّ الَّذِينَ اخْتَلَفُوا فِيهِ لَفِي شَكٍّ مِنْهُ مَا لَهُمْ بِهِ مِنْ عِلْمٍ إِلَّا اتِّبَاعَ الظَّنِّ وَمَا قَتَلُوهُ يَقِينًا (157) بَلْ رَفَعَهُ اللَّهُ إِلَيْهِ وَكَانَ اللَّهُ عَزِيزًا حَكِيمًا. النساء 157-158

Yet the Quran does not deny the death of Christ before His ascension: "When Allah said: O Jesus! I will cause you to die and ascend you to My presence and clear you of those who disbelieve…" (Al-Imran 3:55).

إِذْ قَالَ اللَّهُ يَا عِيسَى إِنِّي مُتَوَفِّيكَ وَرَافِعُكَ إِلَيَّ وَمُطَهِّرُكَ مِنَ الَّذِينَ كَفَرُوا وَجَاعِلُ الَّذِينَ اتَّبَعُوكَ فَوْقَ الَّذِينَ كَفَرُوا إِلَى يَوْمِ الْقِيَامَةِ ثُمَّ إِلَيَّ مَرْجِعُكُمْ فَأَحْكُمُ بَيْنَكُمْ فِيمَا كُنْتُمْ فِيهِ تَخْتَلِفُونَ . آل عمران 55

"Jesus said, 'I was among them, but when Thou didst cause me to die, Thou art the watcher over them, and thou art witness of all things'" (Al-Maidah 5:117).

وكنت عليم شهيدا ما دمت فيهم فلما توفيتني كنت أنت الرقيب عليهم وأنت على كل شيئ شهيد. المائدة 117

"Jesus said, And Peace on me on the day I was born, and on the day I die, and on the day I am raised to life" (Maryam 19:33).

وَالسَّلَامُ عَلَيَّ يَوْمَ وُلِدْتُ وَيَوْمَ أَمُوتُ وَيَوْمَ أُبْعَثُ حَيًّا . مريم 33

However, neither the Quran nor the Muslim scholars have determined or agreed on the way in which Jesus died. Some say that the word "die" or "dead" means asleep, while others say that Jesus died literally.

Who Could Take Christ's Place?

There are many stories in the tradition books of Islam, Al Ahadeeth, as to who it was that was crucified in Jesus' place on the cross. Muslim scholars offered various explanations as to who this person was:

- A Roman guard.

- One of Jesus' disciples who wanted to die instead of Christ, as Jesus promised him a place in paradise.
- Judas, the disciple who betrayed Jesus.
- God put the likeness of Christ on another man who was with Christ.

Killing an innocent man by law is not compatible with a God of mercy and justice. This would be a grossly inequitable act. Such a proposal raises many questions:

1. Since God, the Almighty, is able to do anything, why didn't He raise Christ to Him without the need for killing (or throwing Christ's likeness onto) an innocent man?

2. Being all-powerful, why didn't He blind the soldiers as happened with the prophet Elisha? "And when they (the soldiers' enemies) came down to him, Elisha prayed unto the Lord, and said, 'Smite this people, I pray thee, with blindness.' And He smote them with blindness according to the word of Elisha" (2 Kings 6:18).

3. Why did He not send fire from heaven to consume His enemies as happened with Elijah? "And Elijah answered and said to the Captain of fifty, 'If I be a man of God, then let fire come down from heaven and consume thee and thy fifty'" (2 Kings 1:10).

4. Was Christ not able to deliver Himself from death? He said to the Apostle Peter, one of His disciples, who wanted to use the power of the sword, "Put up again thy sword unto his place, for all they that take the sword shall perish with the sword. Thinkest thou that I cannot now pray to my Father,

and He shall presently give me more than twelve legions of angels? But how then, shall the scriptures be fulfilled, that thus it must be?" (Matthew 26:52-54).

Testimonies of the Crucifixion

Since Muslim scholars and Muslims have not yet come to agreement on the way in which Jesus died, let us go to the original story as described in the Bible. The fundamental teaching of the Bible is that Jesus Christ died on the cross and rose again.

The Apostle Paul said: "For I delivered unto you first of all that which I also received, how that Christ died for our sins according to the scriptures" (1 Corinthians 15:3-4). "But we preach Christ crucified…" (1 Corinthians 1:23).

This Gospel was preached before the time of Muhammad in several parts of the world in different languages, and many accepted and believed it. There is much evidence in numerous historical documents to prove that Jesus was actually crucified:

1. The testimony of the Gospel as seen by different writers:

    "And they crucified Him, and parted His garments, casting lots that it might be fulfilled which was spoken by the prophets. They parted my garments among them, and upon my vesture did they cast lots" (Matthew 27:35).

    "And it was the third hour, and they crucified Him" (Mark 15:25).

"And when they were come to the place which is called Calvary, there they crucified Him, and the malefactors, one on the right hand, and the other on the left" (Luke 23:33).

"Where they crucified Him, and two others with Him, on either side one, and Jesus in the midst" (John 19:18).

2. The apostles' testimony:

    The Apostle Peter said to the Jews: "Him, (Christ) being delivered by the determinate counsel and foreknowledge of God, ye have taken, and by wicked hands have crucified and slain" (Acts 2:23).

    The Apostle Paul said, "Which none of the princes of this world knew, for had they known it, they would not have crucified the Lord of glory" (1 Corinthians 2:6).

    The Apostle John said, "And if we walk in the light, as He is in the light, we have fellowship one with another, and the blood of Jesus Christ His Son cleanseth us from all sin" (1 John 1:7).

3. The testimony of Jesus:

    The Lord Jesus Christ told His disciples of His forthcoming death, and told them that He must die according to the Scriptures: "From that time forth began Jesus to show unto His disciples, how that He must go unto Jerusalem, and suffer many things of the elders and chief priests, and scribes, and be killed, and be raised again the third day" (Matthew 16:21).

"And while they abode in Galilee, Jesus said unto them, The Son of man shall be betrayed into the hands of men: and they shall kill Him, and the third day He shall be raised again…" (Matthew 17:22-23).

"Ye know that after two days is the feast of the Passover, and the Son of man is betrayed to be crucified" (Matthew 26:2).

"And He began to teach them that the Son of man must suffer many things, and be rejected of the elders, and of the chief priests, and scribes, and be killed, and after three days rise again" (Mark 8:31).

"For He taught His disciples, and said unto them, 'The Son of man is delivered into the hands of men, and they shall kill Him: and after that He is killed, He shall rise the third day'" (Mark 9:31).

"Saying, Behold, we go up to Jerusalem; and the Son of man shall be delivered unto the chief priests, and unto the scribes; and they shall condemn Him to death, and shall deliver Him to the Gentiles: and they shall mock Him, and shall scourge Him, and shall spit upon Him, and shall kill Him: and the third day He shall rise again" (Mark 10:33-34).

"Saying, The Son of man must suffer many things, and be rejected of the elders, and chief priests, and scribes, and be slain, and be raised the third day" (Luke 9:22).

"And as Moses lifted up the serpent in the wilderness, even so must the Son of man be lifted up: that whosoever believeth in Him should not perish, but have eternal life" (John 3:14-15).

4. The testimony of the Jews in their Talmud, issued in 1943 (page 42) says that Jesus was crucified a day before the Passover.

5. The events which happened when Jesus was crucified and when He gave up His spirit:

"And, behold, the veil of the temple was rent in twain from the top to the bottom; and the earth did quake, and the rocks rent; and the graves were opened; and many bodies of the saints which slept arose, and came out of the graves after His resurrection, and went into the holy city, and appeared unto many. Now when the centurion and they that were with him, watching Jesus, saw the earthquake, and those things that were done, they feared greatly, saying, 'Truly this was the Son of God'" (Matthew 27:51-54).

"And when the sixth hour was come, there was darkness over the whole land until the ninth hour. And at the ninth hour Jesus cried with a loud voice, saying, "Eloi, Eloi, lama sabachthani?' which is, being interpreted, 'My God, My God, why hast thou forsaken me?' And some of them that stood by, when they heard it, said 'Behold, he calleth Elias.' And ran and filled a sponge full of vinegar, and put it on a reed, and gave it to Him to drink, saying, 'Let alone; let us see whether Elias will come to take Him down.' And Jesus cried with a loud voice, and gave up the ghost. And the veil of the temple was rent in twain from the top to the bottom. And when the centurion, which stood over against Him, saw that He so cried out and gave up the ghost, he said, 'Truly this man was the Son of God'" (Mark 15:33-39).

"And it was about the sixth hour, and there was a darkness over all the earth until the ninth hour. And the sun was darkened, and the veil of the temple was rent in the midst. And when Jesus had cried with a loud voice, He said, 'Father, into Thy hands I commend my spirit,' and having said thus, He gave up the ghost. Now when the centurion saw what was done, he glorified God, saying, 'Certainly this was a righteous man.' And all the people that came together to that sight, beholding the things which were done, smote their breasts, and returned" (Luke 23:44-48).

6. The testimony of history: Many ancient historians, both pagan and Jew, recorded the crucifixion of Jesus in their books. These are a few of the most well known:

    - Tacitus, the pagan, in 55 A.D.
    - Josephus, the Jew, who was born several years after the crucifixion.
    - Lucion, the Greek, in 100 A.D.

7. Christians themselves are not ashamed to believe that Jesus was crucified, and are proud to carry the symbol of the Cross.

It seems absurd that somebody who came several hundred years after the event should attempt to deny the facts of the crucifixion when he was not present to witness its occurrence. If even the enemies of Christianity at the time should give evidence that the crucifixion of Jesus Christ took place, what reason would anybody have in wanting to deny it?

Some sincere Muslims who wish to see harmony between Christianity and Islam state that if Christians were to give up their belief in the crucifixion, both religions and beliefs could become one. However, the Christian's answer is surely to say that there would be no Christianity without the cross.

The Apostle Paul said: "And if Christ be not risen, then is our preaching in vain…" (1 Corinthians 15:14).

WHY THE CROSS? لماذا الصليب

While walking with a friend one day beside a small lake, enjoying the sunlight glittering on the water, the flowers and the green grass, and thinking of the Creator who had made all these wonderful things, he turned to me and asked, "Why the Cross? I mean, why did Jesus choose the cross to be the way of salvation? Surely He could have chosen another way to save the world from its sin!"

This was an important question. An omnipotent God could surely have chosen to avoid the suffering of the crucifixion.

How do we answer such a question?

Planned From the Beginning

1. In the beginning, when God created man, He did so for His pleasure. In the book of Revelation, we read: "Thou art worthy, O Lord to receive glory, honor, and power: for thou

hast created all things, and for thy pleasure they are created and were created" (Revelation 4:11). God did not create man as a machine then leave it to run by itself.

2. When Adam fell in his sin, God in His love did not destroy him but found a scapegoat that could be destroyed in Adam's place. This was the first symbol of sacrifice. "…The Lord God made coats of skin, and clothed them" (Genesis 3:21). This was the beginning of God's plan for an everlasting sacrifice, one and for all.

3. The shedding of blood was necessary for the forgiveness of sins. "And almost all things are by the law purged with blood; and without the shedding of blood is no remission" (Hebrews 9:22).

4. The blood of animals was not sufficient to fully take away sin, however. "For it is not possible that the blood of bulls and of goats should take away sins" (Hebrews 10:4).

5. Although God is omnipotent, He does not always show His power in a physical way. He could have saved mankind with a simple word from His mouth, but He wanted to show His love to His creatures, and to bring man into close fellowship with Himself (to reconcile man to God). "For if, when we were enemies, we were reconciled to God by the death of His Son, much more, being reconciled, we shall be saved by His life" (Romans 5:10).

Jesus said to Peter that He could use power. "Thinkest thou that I cannot now pray to my Father, and He shall presently give me more than twelve legions of angels? But how then shall the Scriptures be fulfilled, that thus it must be?" (Matthew 26:52-54).

6. A true scapegoat had to be provided for man, a person without sin, a solvent to the debt of Heaven. "For the wages of sin is death" (Romans 6:23). This had to take the place of many insufficient sacrifices.

7. Jesus Christ, the Word of God, had to become the scapegoat and to take on the image of man, to be made the everlasting sacrifice. "But made Himself of no reputation, and took upon Him the form of a servant, and was made in the likeness of men" (Philippians 2:7).

8. The cross was an obnoxious way of punishment. It was seen as a curse, not only by the government at the time (the Romans), but also by the enemies of the Jews, as well as by the Jews themselves. It was the worst possible way for a man to be punished. "...Cursed is everyone that hangeth on a tree" (Deuteronomy 21:23).

9. The cross had been planned from the very beginning as a way of salvation for man. God ordained a means of sacrifice for Adam, Isaac, and the people of Israel throughout their history. These sacrifices were merely a symbol of the greater everlasting sacrifice to come, Jesus Christ. The cross was the sign of a curse, while the blood was the way of salvation from that curse. "Christ hath redeemed us from the curse of the cross, being made a curse for us, for it is written, Cursed is everyone that hangeth on a tree" (Galatians 3:13).

10. An intercessor was needed to stand between God the Holy One, and man the sinner, to reconcile man to God, and to bring him into a holy relationship with God. The coming of Christ to earth and dwelling in the flesh to save mankind is

more meaningful to man than the sending of an angel. "But though we, or an angel from heaven, preach any other gospel unto you than that which we have preached unto you, let him be accursed" (Galatians 1:8).

11. Christ's suffering is more appreciated than using power in order to save mankind. "Surely He hath borne our griefs, and carried our sorrows: Yet we did esteem Him stricken, smitten of God, and afflicted. But He was wounded for our transgressions, He was bruised for our iniquities: The chastisement of our peace was upon Him; and with His stripes we are healed" (Isaiah 53:4-5).

12. In His suffering as a man, Jesus experienced, and overcame, all things that man would ever suffer. Because He overcame even death itself, the ultimate consequence of sin, those who look to Him are given the strength to overcome: "For that He Himself suffered being tempted, He is able to succour them that are tempted" (Hebrews 2:18).

THE BIBLE الكتاب المقدس

For those who follow the Quran, accusations regarding the alteration of the Bible undermine their own teachings and the credibility of the Quran itself. They invade the Bible, forgetting the Quran has endorsed it. If the Quran endorses and acts as guardian to the Bible, dispute over the alteration of the script of the Bible is absurd.

"And we have sent after them in their footsteps Jesus, son of Mary, verifying what was before him of the Torah, and we gave him the Gospel, in which was guidance and light and verifying what was before it of the Torah, and a guidance and an admonition for those who guard…And we have revealed to you the book (Quran) with the truth, verifying what is before it of the Book (Bible) and a guardian over it…" (Al Maidah 5:46-48).

وَقَفَّيْنَا عَلَى آثَارِهِم بِعِيسَى ابْنِ مَرْيَمَ مُصَدِّقًا لِمَا بَيْنَ يَدَيْهِ مِنَ التَّوْرَاةِ وَآتَيْنَاهُ الْإِنْجِيلَ فِيهِ هُدًى وَنُورٌ وَمُصَدِّقًا لِمَا بَيْنَ يَدَيْهِ مِنَ التَّوْرَاةِ وَهُدًى وَمَوْعِظَةً لِلْمُتَّقِينَ (46) وَلْيَحْكُمْ أَهْلُ الْإِنْجِيلِ بِمَا أَنزَلَ اللَّهُ فِيهِ وَمَن لَّمْ يَحْكُم بِمَا أَنزَلَ اللَّهُ فَأُولَٰئِكَ هُمُ الْفَاسِقُونَ (47) وَأَنزَلْنَا إِلَيْكَ الْكِتَابَ بِالْحَقِّ مُصَدِّقًا لِمَا بَيْنَ يَدَيْهِ مِنَ الْكِتَابِ

وَمُهَيْمِنًا عَلَيْهِ
فَاحْكُمْ بَيْنَهُمْ بِمَا أَنْزَلَ اللَّهُ وَلَا تَتَّبِعْ أَهْوَاءَهُمْ عَمَّا جَاءَكَ مِنَ الْحَقِّ لِكُلٍّ جَعَلْنَا مِنْكُمْ شِرْعَةً وَمِنْهَاجًا وَلَوْ شَاءَ اللَّهُ لَجَعَلَكُمْ أُمَّةً وَاحِدَةً وَلَكِنْ لِيَبْلُوَكُمْ فِي مَا آتَاكُمْ فَاسْتَبِقُوا الْخَيْرَاتِ إِلَى اللَّهِ مَرْجِعُكُمْ جَمِيعًا فَيُنَبِّئُكُمْ بِمَا كُنْتُمْ فِيهِ تَخْتَلِفُونَ . المائدة 46-48

In order to accept whether the Biblical writings were distorted, we have to ask those who claim such allegations these questions:

1. When was the Bible distorted?

   It was an embarrassment to those who said that alteration of the Bible took place before Muhammad, as they forgot that Muhammad confirmed the truth of the Bible, and drew his people's attention to it as a confirmation of his call. "But if you are in doubt as to what We have revealed to you, ask those who read the Book (Bible) before you…" (Yunus 10:94).

   فَإِنْ كُنْتَ فِي شَكٍّ مِمَّا أَنْزَلْنَا إِلَيْكَ فَاسْأَلِ الَّذِينَ يَقْرَءُونَ الْكِتَابَ مِنْ قَبْلِكَ لَقَدْ جَاءَكَ الْحَقُّ مِنْ رَبِّكَ فَلَا تَكُونَنَّ مِنَ الْمُمْتَرِينَ . يونس 94

   Verses such as this made them change their minds and say that the alteration took place after the time of Muhammad.

   One could ask, "Is it easier to catch one bird in a cage or ten in a tree?" Until recently, the Quran was written in one language only Arabic: "And this is a book in Arabic…" (Al-Ahqaf 46:12).

   وَمِنْ قَبْلِهِ كِتَابُ مُوسَى إِمَامًا وَرَحْمَةً وَهَذَا كِتَابٌ مُصَدِّقٌ لِسَانًا عَرَبِيًّا لِيُنْذِرَ الَّذِينَ ظَلَمُوا وَبُشْرَى لِلْمُحْسِنِينَ . الاحقاف 12

   However, the Bible was translated into several languages and distributed to many countries even before the Quran. Who could possibly have been ingenious enough to have collected all the copies of the Bible from across the world and make an identical alteration in each of them?

2. Who, if anyone, distorted the Bible?

If Christians had at any time distorted the Bible, how did they manage this? Also, their Book warns them of serious consequences if anyone changes the Book. "For I testify unto every man that heareth the words of the prophesy of this book, if any man shall add unto these things, God shall add unto him the plagues that are written in this book: And if any man shall take away from the words of the book of this prophecy, God shall take away his part out of the book of life, and out of the holy city, and from the things which are written in this book" (Revelation 22:18-19).

Where were the Jews at that time? Couldn't they do something to stop their enemies, the Christians, from changing their holy book, the Torah?

If we were to postulate that a joint league of Jews and Christians had distorted the Bible, why was such an incident not recorded historically? Was it possible that even one original copy was hidden away by a faithful Christian to avoid being changed?

Some believed that translation from the original language means alteration; if this is true, this will include any translation of the Quran as well. The Bible has been translated throughout the centuries, but the fundamental truth remains the same.

A deep study of the Bible reveals that both the Old and the New Testaments convey the same message—that God planned man's salvation from the very beginning, through the person of the Lord Jesus Christ.

3. The Quran is supposed to be a "Guardian" over the Bible. "And we have revealed to you the book (Quran) with the truth, verifying what is before it of the Book (Bible) and a guardian over it…" (Al-Maidah 5:48).

وَأَنْزَلْنَا إِلَيْكَ الْكِتَابَ بِالْحَقِّ مُصَدِّقًا لِمَا بَيْنَ يَدَيْهِ مِنَ الْكِتَابِ وَمُهَيْمِنًا عَلَيْهِ فَاحْكُمْ بَيْنَهُمْ بِمَا أَنْزَلَ اللَّهُ وَلَا تَتَّبِعْ أَهْوَاءَهُمْ عَمَّا جَاءَكَ مِنَ الْحَقِّ لِكُلٍّ جَعَلْنَا مِنْكُمْ شِرْعَةً وَمِنْهَاجًا وَلَوْ شَاءَ اللَّهُ لَجَعَلَكُمْ أُمَّةً وَاحِدَةً وَلَكِنْ لِيَبْلُوَكُمْ فِي مَا آتَاكُمْ فَاسْتَبِقُوا الْخَيْرَاتِ إِلَى اللَّهِ مَرْجِعُكُمْ جَمِيعًا فَيُنَبِّئُكُمْ بِمَا كُنْتُمْ فِيهِ تَخْتَلِفُونَ . المائدة 48

If this is so, any alleged alterations of the Bible must be blamed on the Quran, which failed to fulfill its responsibility in protecting the Bible.

The Bible in the Quran

1. We find in the Quranic verse that the Quran is Muhammad's original message. Allah says to Muhammad, "But if you are in doubt as to what We have revealed to you, ask those who read the Book (Bible) before you" (Yunus 10:94).

فَإِنْ كُنْتَ فِي شَكٍّ مِمَّا أَنْزَلْنَا إِلَيْكَ فَاسْأَلِ الَّذِينَ يَقْرَءُونَ الْكِتَابَ مِنْ قَبْلِكَ لَقَدْ جَاءَكَ الْحَقُّ مِنْ رَبِّكَ فَلَا تَكُونَنَّ مِنَ الْمُمْتَرِينَ . يونس 94

2. The Quran confirms the Bible. "He has revealed to you the book (Quran) with truth, verifying that which is before it (Bible)" (Al-Imran 3:3).

نَزَّلَ عَلَيْكَ الْكِتَابَ بِالْحَقِّ مُصَدِّقًا لِمَا بَيْنَ يَدَيْهِ وَأَنْزَلَ التَّوْرَاةَ وَالْإِنْجِيلَ . آل عمران 3

3. The Quran surrenders to it. "Say: We believe in Allah and in that which has been revealed to us, and in that which was revealed to Abraham and Ishmael and Isaac and Jacob and the tribes, and in that which was given to Moses and Jesus, and in that which was given to the prophets for their Lord; we do not distinguish between any of them, and to it do we submit" (Al-Baqarah 2:136).

قُولُوا آمَنَّا بِاللَّهِ وَمَا أُنْزِلَ إِلَيْنَا وَمَا أُنْزِلَ إِلَى إِبْرَاهِيمَ وَإِسْمَاعِيلَ وَإِسْحَاقَ وَيَعْقُوبَ وَالْأَسْبَاطِ وَمَا أُوتِيَ مُوسَى وَعِيسَى وَمَا أُوتِيَ النَّبِيُّونَ مِنْ رَبِّهِمْ لَا نُفَرِّقُ بَيْنَ أَحَدٍ مِنْهُمْ وَنَحْنُ لَهُ مُسْلِمُونَ . البقرة 136

4. The Quran should protect it. "...And a guardian over it..." (Al-Maidah 5:48).

وَأَنْزَلْنَا إِلَيْكَ الْكِتَابَ بِالْحَقِّ مُصَدِّقًا لِمَا بَيْنَ يَدَيْهِ مِنَ الْكِتَابِ وَمُهَيْمِنًا عَلَيْهِ فَاحْكُمْ بَيْنَهُمْ بِمَا أَنْزَلَ اللَّهُ وَلَا تَتَّبِعْ أَهْوَاءَهُمْ عَمَّا جَاءَكَ مِنَ الْحَقِّ لِكُلٍّ جَعَلْنَا مِنْكُمْ شِرْعَةً وَمِنْهَاجًا وَلَوْ شَاءَ اللَّهُ لَجَعَلَكُمْ أُمَّةً وَاحِدَةً وَلَكِنْ لِيَبْلُوَكُمْ فِي مَا آتَاكُمْ فَاسْتَبِقُوا الْخَيْرَاتِ إِلَى اللَّهِ مَرْجِعُكُمْ جَمِيعًا فَيُنَبِّئُكُمْ بِمَا كُنْتُمْ فِيهِ تَخْتَلِفُونَ . المائدة 48

5. The Bible is a guide and a light. "And We have him (Jesus) the Gospel, in which was guidance and light..." (Al-Maidah 5:46).

وَقَفَّيْنَا عَلَى آثَارِهِمْ بِعِيسَى ابْنِ مَرْيَمَ مُصَدِّقًا لِمَا بَيْنَ يَدَيْهِ مِنَ التَّوْرَاةِ وَآتَيْنَاهُ الْإِنْجِيلَ فِيهِ هُدًى وَنُورٌ وَمُصَدِّقًا لِمَا بَيْنَ يَدَيْهِ مِنَ التَّوْرَاةِ وَهُدًى وَمَوْعِظَةً لِلْمُتَّقِينَ الْفَاسِقُونَ . المائدة 46

6. The Bible is a Judge. "And how do they make you a judge and they have the Torah wherein is Allah's judgment?" (Al-Maidah 5:43).

وَكَيْفَ يُحَكِّمُونَكَ وَعِنْدَهُمُ التَّوْرَاةُ فِيهَا حُكْمُ اللَّهِ ثُمَّ يَتَوَلَّوْنَ مِنْ بَعْدِ ذَلِكَ وَمَا أُولَئِكَ بِالْمُؤْمِنِينَ . المائدة 43

7. The Quran commands Christians to fulfill the Bible. "Say, O Followers of the Book! You follow no good till you keep up the Torah and the Gospel and that which is revealed to you from your Lord" (Al-Maidah 5:68).

قُلْ يَا أَهْلَ الْكِتَابِ لَسْتُمْ عَلَى شَيْءٍ حَتَّى تُقِيمُوا التَّوْرَاةَ وَالإِنْجِيلَ وَمَا أُنْزِلَ إِلَيْكُمْ مِنْ رَبِّكُمْ وَلَيَزِيدَنَّ كَثِيرًا مِنْهُمْ مَا أُنْزِلَ إِلَيْكَ مِنْ رَبِّكَ طُغْيَانًا وَكُفْرًا فَلَا تَأْسَ عَلَى الْقَوْمِ الْكَافِرِينَ . المائدة 68

8. All people, including Muslims, are to believe in the Bible. "O you who believe! Believe in Allah and His Apostle and the Book which has revealed to His Apostle and the Book which He revealed before" (Al-Nisa 4:136).

يَا أَيُّهَا الَّذِينَ آمَنُوا آمِنُوا بِاللَّهِ وَرَسُولِهِ وَالْكِتَابِ الَّذِي نَزَّلَ عَلَى رَسُولِهِ وَالْكِتَابِ الَّذِي أَنْزَلَ مِنْ قَبْلُ وَمَنْ يَكْفُرْ بِاللَّهِ وَمَلَائِكَتِهِ وَكُتُبِهِ وَرُسُلِهِ وَالْيَوْمِ الْآخِرِ فَقَدْ ضَلَّ ضَلَالًا بَعِيدًا . النساء 136

The Bible is a mercy: "Before it was the Book of Moses, a guide and a mercy" (Al-Ahqaf 46:12).

وَمِنْ قَبْلِهِ كِتَابُ مُوسَى إِمَامًا وَرَحْمَةً وَهَذَا كِتَابٌ مُصَدِّقٌ لِسَانًا عَرَبِيًّا لِيُنْذِرَ الَّذِينَ ظَلَمُوا وَبُشْرَى لِلْمُحْسِنِينَ . الاحقاف 12

THE INFALLIBILITY OF THE BIBLE

عصمة الكتاب المقدس

Biblical Evidence

1. God Himself has promised that He will not change His word as we read in the Old Testament. "My covenant will I not break, nor alter the things that are gone out of my lips" (Psalms 89:34).

   And we find also in the New Testament that Jesus said: "Heaven and earth shall pass away, but my words shall not pass away" (Matthew 24:35).

2. Isaiah, the prophet had declared the same fact: "The grass withereth, the flower fadeth; but the Word of our God shall stand forever" (Isaiah 40:8).

"Seek ye out of the book of the Lord, and read: No one of these shall fail, none shall want her mate; for my mouth it hath commanded, and his spirit it hath gathered them" (Isaiah 34:16).

3. The disciples gave their statement also of the unchangeable scriptures. "But the Word of the Lord endureth forever. And this is the Word which by the gospel is preached unto you" (1 Peter 1:25).

   "We have also a more sure Word of prophecy; where unto ye do well that ye take heed, as unto a light that shineth in a dark place, until the day dawn, and the day star arise in your hearts: Knowing this first, that no prophecy of the scripture is of any private interpretation. For the prophecy came not in old time by the will of man, but holy men of God spake as they were moved by the Holy Ghost" (2 Peter 1:19-21).

4. "That which was from the beginning, which we have heard, which we have seen with our eyes, which we have looked upon, and our hands have handled, of the Word of life" (1 John 1:1).

5. "All scripture is given by inspiration of God, and is profitable for doctrine, for reproof, for correction, for instruction in righteousness" (2 Timothy 3:16).

Quranic Evidence

The Quran also testifies that God's Word cannot be changed.

1. "And there is none to change the word of Allah" (Al-An'am 6:34).

وَلَقَدْ كُذِّبَتْ رُسُلٌ مِنْ قَبْلِكَ فَصَبَرُوا عَلَى مَا كُذِّبُوا وَأُوذُوا حَتَّى أَتَاهُمْ نَصْرُنَا وَلَا مُبَدِّلَ لِكَلِمَاتِ اللَّهِ وَلَقَدْ جَاءَكَ مِنْ نَبَإِ الْمُرْسَلِينَ . الإنعام 34

2. "There is none who can change His word" (Al-An'am 6:115).

وَتَمَّتْ كَلِمَةُ رَبِّكَ صِدْقًا وَعَدْلًا لَا مُبَدِّلَ لِكَلِمَاتِهِ وَهُوَ السَّمِيعُ الْعَلِيمُ . الإنعام 115

3. God protects His Word. "Surely We have revealed the Reminder and We will most surely be its guardian" (Al-Hajar 15:9).

إِنَّا نَحْنُ نَزَّلْنَا الذِّكْرَ وَإِنَّا لَهُ لَحَافِظُون . الحجر 9

Historical Evidence

Let us come now to the historical evidence of the authenticity of the Bible. There are several copies of the Bible on display in the museums of the world, some of which were written before and some after the life of Muhammad. These copies are the same as the ones used by Christians today in different languages around the world.

1. The Codex Alexandrianus at the British Museum in London was written about 325 A.D. in Greek.

2. The Codex Vaticanus at the Vatican library in Rome was written about 300 A.D. in Greek and contains the whole bible.

3. The Codex Ephraimi, kept in the Paris Museum in France, was written in Greek about 450 A.D.

4. The Codex Sinaiticus was discovered by the German scholar Teshindorf in 1844. It is kept at the British Museum in London.

With references available to all these Bibles, it can be seen that any allegation of distortion of the Bible is groundless. Through the times of persecution of Christians throughout the ages, God has seen provident to protect His Word against any maltreatment or distortion, for He is a vigilant God.

My dear Muslim friends, my advice to you is that you should now turn to the Quran, which commends you to search the Bible, the Word of Truth that never changes. The writer of the book of Psalms says that the Word of God is everything to him. Here are some Biblical quotations of his own experience:

> "How sweet are the Thy words unto my taste! Yea, sweeter than honey to my mouth. Through Thy precepts I get understanding: therefore I hate every false way. Thy Word is a lamp unto my feet, and a light unto my path" (Psalms 119:103-105).

> "Thy testimonies have I taken as a heritage forever: for they are the rejoicing of my heart" (Psalms 119:111).

> "Thy testimonies are wonderful: therefore doth my soul keep them. The entrance of thy words giveth light; it giveth understanding unto the simple" (Psalms 119:129-130).

> "Righteous art Thou, O Lord, and upright are Thy judgments" (Psalms 119:137).

"Thy righteousness is an everlasting righteousness, and Thy law is the truth" (Psalms 119:142).

"Concerning Thy testimonies, I have known of old that Thou hast founded them forever" (Psalms 119:152).

"Thy Word is true from the beginning: and every one of Thy righteous judgments endureth forever" (Psalms 119:160).

"I rejoice at Thy Word, as one that findeth great spoil. I hate and abhor lying: but Thy law do I love. Seven times a day do I praise Thee, because of Thy righteous judgments" (Psalms 119:162-164).

Jesus also promised, "If ye abide in me, and my words abide in you, ye shall ask what ye will, and it shall be done unto you" (John 15:7).

LOVE المحبة

The Muslims say that the divine names of Allah are ninety-nine, which are recorded on the palm of our hands. Examples of these names are "Great," "High," and "Holy." But one name that is not mentioned is "God is Love." God's love in the Quran is limited to good people only, and is not freely given.

"…Then surely Allah loves those who guard against evil" (Al-Imran 3:76).

بَلَى مَنْ أَوْفَى بِعَهْدِهِ وَاتَّقَى فَإِنَّ اللَّهَ يُحِبُّ الْمُتَّقِينَ . آل عمران 76

"…Surely, Allah loves those who are careful" (Al-Tauba 9:4).

إِلا الَّذِينَ عَاهَدْتُمْ مِنَ الْمُشْرِكِينَ ثُمَّ لَمْ يَنْقُصُوكُمْ شَيْئًا وَلَمْ يُظَاهِرُوا عَلَيْكُمْ أَحَدًا فَأَتِمُّوا إِلَيْهِمْ عَهْدَهُمْ إِلَى مُدَّتِهِمْ إِنَّ اللَّهَ يُحِبُّ الْمُتَّقِينَ . التوبة 4

"…Surely Allah loves the doers of good" (Al-Baqarah 2:195).

وَأَنْفِقُوا فِي سَبِيلِ اللَّهِ وَلا تُلْقُوا بِأَيْدِيكُمْ إِلَى التَّهْلُكَةِ وَأَحْسِنُوا إِنَّ اللَّهَ يُحِبُّ الْمُحْسِنِينَ . البقرة 195

"...And Allah loves the patient" (Al-Imran 3:146).

وَكَأَيِّنْ مِنْ نَبِيٍّ قَاتَلَ مَعَهُ رِبِّيُّونَ كَثِيرٌ فَمَا وَهَنُوا لِمَا أَصَابَهُمْ فِي سَبِيلِ اللَّهِ وَمَا ضَعُفُوا وَمَا اسْتَكَانُوا وَاللَّهُ يُحِبُّ الصَّابِرِينَ. آل عمران 146

God as He Is

The Bible speaks of God differently, saying, "He <u>is</u> Love."

> "And we have known and believed the love that God hath to us. God is love; and he that dwelleth in love dwelleth in God, and God in him" (1 John 4:16).

> "Herein is love, not that we loved God, but that He loved us, and sent His Son to be the propitiation for our sins" (1 John 4:10).

God is Holy; He hates sin, but He loves even sinners and desires to save them from their sin. "But God commendeth His love towards us, in that while we were yet sinners, Christ died for us" (Romans 5:8).

Man's Love for Others

Man's love in the Quran is basically for those who love him, but is not applicable to enemies, especially those who are from another faith. Those who do not follow the way of Islam should be killed, according to Quranic teaching.

> "...Then slay the idolaters wherever you find them, and take them captives and besiege them, and lie in wait for them in every ambush" (Al-Tauba 9:5).

فَإِذَا انْسَلَخَ الْأَشْهُرُ الْحُرُمُ فَاقْتُلُوا الْمُشْرِكِينَ حَيْثُ وَجَدْتُمُوهُمْ وَخُذُوهُمْ وَاحْصُرُوهُمْ وَاقْعُدُوا لَهُمْ كُلَّ مَرْصَدٍ فَإِنْ تَابُوا وَأَقَامُوا الصَّلَاةَ وَآتَوُا الزَّكَاةَ فَخَلُّوا سَبِيلَهُمْ إِنَّ اللَّهَ غَفُورٌ رَحِيمٌ . التوبة 5

"Fight those who do not believe in Allah, nor in the latter day, nor do they prohibit what Allah and His Apostle have prohibited, nor follow the religion of truth, out of those who have been given the book (Bible), until they pay the tax in acknowledgment of superiority and they are in a state of subjection" (Al-Tauba 9:29).

قَاتِلُوا الَّذِينَ لَا يُؤْمِنُونَ بِاللَّهِ وَلَا بِالْيَوْمِ الْآخِرِ وَلَا يُحَرِّمُونَ مَا حَرَّمَ اللَّهُ وَرَسُولُهُ وَلَا يَدِينُونَ دِينَ الْحَقِّ مِنَ الَّذِينَ أُوتُوا الْكِتَابَ حَتَّى يُعْطُوا الْجِزْيَةَ عَنْ يَدٍ وَهُمْ صَاغِرُونَ . التوبة 29

"And if you take your turn, then retaliate with the like of that with which you were afflicted" (Al-Nahl 16:125).

وَإِنْ عَاقَبْتُمْ فَعَاقِبُوا بِمِثْلِ مَا عُوقِبْتُمْ بِهِ وَلَئِنْ صَبَرْتُمْ لَهُوَ خَيْرٌ لِلصَّابِرِينَ . النحل 125

"O Prophet! Urge the believers to war" (Al-Anfal 8:65).

يَا أَيُّهَا النَّبِيُّ حَرِّضِ الْمُؤْمِنِينَ عَلَى الْقِتَالِ إِنْ يَكُنْ مِنْكُمْ عِشْرُونَ صَابِرُونَ يَغْلِبُوا مِائَتَيْنِ وَإِنْ يَكُنْ مِنْكُمْ مِائَةٌ يَغْلِبُوا أَلْفًا مِنَ الَّذِينَ كَفَرُوا بِأَنَّهُمْ قَوْمٌ لَا يَفْقَهُونَ . الانفال 65

"And fight in the way of Allah with those who fight with you" (Al-Baqarah 2:190).

وقاتلوا في سبيل الله الذين يقاتلونكم. البقرة 190

"And We prescribe to them in it that life is for life, and eye for eye, and nose for nose, and ear for ear, and tooth for tooth…" (Al-Maidah 5:45).

وَكَتَبْنَا عَلَيْهِمْ فِيهَا أَنَّ النَّفْسَ بِالنَّفْسِ وَالْعَيْنَ بِالْعَيْنِ وَالْأَنْفَ بِالْأَنْفِ وَالْأُذُنَ بِالْأُذُنِ وَالسِّنَّ بِالسِّنِّ وَالْجُرُوحَ قِصَاصٌ فَمَنْ تَصَدَّقَ بِهِ فَهُوَ كَفَّارَةٌ لَهُ وَمَنْ لَمْ يَحْكُمْ بِمَا أَنْزَلَ اللَّهُ فَأُولَئِكَ هُمُ الظَّالِمُونَ . المائدة 45

"Therefore, take not from among them (unbelievers) friends until they fly in Allah's way; but if they turn back, then seize them and kill them wherever you find them; and take not from among them a friend or a helper" (Al-Nisa 4:89).

وَدُّوا لَوْ تَكْفُرُونَ كَمَا كَفَرُوا فَتَكُونُونَ سَوَاءً فَلَا تَتَّخِذُوا مِنْهُمْ أَوْلِيَاءَ حَتَّى يُهَاجِرُوا فِي سَبِيلِ اللَّهِ فَإِنْ تَوَلَّوْا فَخُذُوهُمْ وَاقْتُلُوهُمْ حَيْثُ وَجَدْتُمُوهُمْ وَلَا تَتَّخِذُوا مِنْهُمْ وَلِيًّا وَلَا نَصِيرًا . النساء 89

The essence of the Bible's teaching goes beyond every teaching, however, in that our love should embrace all mankind, even our enemies.

> Jesus said: "…love your enemies, bless them that curse you, do good to them that hate you, and pray for them which despitefully use you, and persecute you; that ye may be the children of your Father which is in heaven: for he maketh his sun rise on the evil and on the good, and sendeth rain on the just and on the unjust. For if ye love them which love you, what reward have ye? Do not even the publicans the same?" (Matthew 5:44-46).

> "These things I command you, that ye love one another" (John 15:17).

> "But I say unto you, that ye resist not evil: but whosoever shall smite thee on the right cheek, turn to him the other also" (Matthew 5:39).

"A new commandment I give unto you, that ye love one another; as I have loved you, that ye also love one another" (John 13:34).

The Apostles Paul and John, Jesus' followers, write:

"Dearly beloved, avenge not yourselves, but rather give place unto wrath: for it is written, 'Vengeance is mine, I will repay, saith the Lord'" (Romans 12:19).

"But he that hateth his brother is in the darkness and walketh in darkness, and knoweth not whither he goes, because that darkness hath blinded his eyes" (1 John 2:11).

"He that loveth not his brother abideth in death" (1 John 3:14).

The most beautiful chapter in the Bible that describes love, written by the Apostle Paul, is 1 Corinthians chapter 13. In the King James version of the Bible, the word "charity" is used to describe unconditional, self-sacrificing love.

"Though I speak with the tongues of men and of angels, and have not charity, I am become as sounding brass, or a tinkling cymbal. And though I have the gift of prophecy, and understand all mysteries, and all knowledge; and though I have all faith, so that I could remove mountains, and have not charity, I am nothing. And though I bestow all my goods to feed the poor, and though I give my body to be burned, and have not charity, it profiteth me nothing. Charity suffereth long, and is kind; charity envieth not; charity vaunteth not itself, is not puffed up. Doth not behave itself unseemly, seeketh not her own, is not easily provoked, thinketh no evil;

rejoiceth not in iniquity, but rejoiceth in the truth; beareth all things, believeth all things, hopeth all things, endureth all things. Charity never faileth: but whether there be prophecies, they shall fail; whether there be tongues, they shall cease; whether there be knowledge it shall vanish away. For we know in part, and we prophesy in part. But when that which is perfect is come, then that which is in part shall be done away. When I was a child, I spake as a child, I understood as a child, I thought as a child: but when I became a man, I put away childish things. For now we see through a glass, darkly; but then face to face: now I know in part; but then shall I know even as also I am known. And now abideth faith, hope, charity, these three; but the greatest of these is charity" (1 Corinthians 13).

Some mystic Muslims realize this truth, and they are searching for a deeper love for God which is not found in the Quran. The Soufee's paraphrase for the first chapter of the Quran, Sura Al-Fatiha (The Opening): "God lead us to the straight way, lead us to the way that leads us to You, and bless us with Your love which is the essence of Yourself, and set us free from everything that might hinder us from You, and guide us to the way in which we don't see but You, and don't hear but Your voice, and don't love but You."

It is not impossible to have such love. Jesus never commanded us to do what we cannot accomplish, but it is not possible on our own. If you ask Him with all your heart to give you love for others, He will answer your prayers. It will be His own love being expressed through you. Ask Him to create a clean heart within you, for He is able to do so.

FORGIVENESS الغفران

The word "forgiveness" also means "forgetting." It is the result when someone says, "I will not do it again," followed by God's reply, "I will not remember it any longer."

Although the Quran teaches that God is the Forgiver, "Al-Ghaffar," الغفّار man's sins do not disappear but remain until the Day of Judgment when all man's works will be weighed.

> "And the measuring out on that day will be just; then as for him whose measure (of good deeds) is heavy, there are they who shall be successful. And as for him whose measure (of good deeds) is light, there are they who have made their soul suffer loss" (Al-A'Raf 7:8-9).
>
> وَالْوَزْنُ يَوْمَئِذٍ الْحَقُّ فَمَنْ ثَقُلَتْ مَوَازِينُهُ فَأُولَٰئِكَ هُمُ الْمُفْلِحُونَ (8) وَمَنْ خَفَّتْ مَوَازِينُهُ فَأُولَٰئِكَ الَّذِينَ خَسِرُوا أَنْفُسَهُمْ بِمَا كَانُوا بِآيَاتِنَا يَظْلِمُونَ (9) .
> الاعراف 8-9

> "Surely good deeds take away evil deeds…" (Hud 11:114).

وَأَقِمِ الصَّلاةَ طَرَفَيِ النَّهَارِ وَزُلَفًا مِنَ اللَّيْلِ إِنَّ الْحَسَنَاتِ يُذْهِبْنَ السَّيِّئَاتِ ذَلِكَ ذِكْرَى لِلذَّاكِرِينَ . هود 114

But how can God forgive if the sins are still there, and man still has to work hard to cover his bad works? It would seem for the Muslim that forgiveness does not exist.

The Grace of God Versus Man's Good Works

The Bible acknowledges that man originally is not good. The Apostle Paul said, "For I know that in me, that is, in my flesh, dwelleth no good thing" (Romans 7:18).

Forgiveness in the Bible is practical and complete. It is God's part in response to repentance, which is man's part. The Bible says:

> "If we *confess* our sins, He is faithful and just to *forgive* us our sins, and to cleanse us from all unrighteousness" (1 John 1:9, emphasis added).

> "For by *grace* are ye saved through faith; and that not of yourselves: it is the gift of God not of *works*, lest any man should boast" (Ephesians 2:8-9, emphasis added).

> "Blessed is he whose transgression is forgiven, whose sin is covered. Blessed is the man unto whom the Lord imputeth not iniquity, and in whose spirit there is no guile" (Psalms 32:1-2).

> "And the times of this ignorance God winked at..." (Acts 17:30).

"For I will be merciful to their unrighteousness and their sins and their iniquities will I remember no more" (Hebrews 8:12).

"Being justified freely by His grace through the redemption that is in Christ Jesus" (Romans 3:24).

There is no assurance in the Quran that a person will deserve the merit of his good deeds. God has the final decision, and God does what He pleases, even though the good deeds are heavier than the bad deeds.

"Allah sends astray whom He pleases, and He guides whom He pleases" (Ibrahim 14:4).

وَمَا أَرْسَلْنَا مِنْ رَسُولٍ إِلا بِلِسَانِ قَوْمِهِ لِيُبَيِّنَ لَهُمْ فَيُضِلُّ اللَّهُ مَنْ يَشَاءُ وَيَهْدِي مَنْ يَشَاءُ وَهُوَ الْعَزِيزُ الْحَكِيمُ . ابراهيم 4

"He forgives whom He pleases and torments whom He pleases" (Al-Imran 3:129).

وَلِلَّهِ مَا فِي السَّمَوَاتِ وَمَا فِي الْأَرْضِ يَغْفِرُ لِمَنْ يَشَاءُ وَيُعَذِّبُ مَنْ يَشَاءُ وَاللَّهُ غَفُورٌ رَحِيمٌ . آل عمران 129

"...whom Allah pleases, He sends astray, and whom He pleases, He puts on the right way" (Al-An'am 6:39).

وَالَّذِينَ كَذَّبُوا بِآيَاتِنَا صُمٌّ وَبُكْمٌ فِي الظُّلُمَاتِ مَنْ يَشَإِ اللَّهُ يُضْلِلْهُ وَمَنْ يَشَأْ يَجْعَلْهُ عَلَى صِرَاطٍ مُسْتَقِيمٍ الإنعام 39

In contrast, what a wonderful assurance we have in the Bible.

Jesus said, "Let not your heart be troubled...I will come again, and receive you unto myself; that where I am, there ye may be also" (John 14:1,3).

"And being fully persuaded that, what He had promised, He was also able to perform" (Romans 4:21).

"For the Scripture saith, Whosoever believeth on Him shall not be ashamed. For whosoever shall call upon the name of the Lord shall be saved" (Romans 10:11-12).

"…But we know that when He shall appear, we shall be like Him, for we shall see Him as He is" (1 John 3:2).

"…For I know whom I have believed, and am persuaded that He is able to keep that which I have committed unto Him against that day" (2 Timothy 1:12).

"And this is the will of Him that sent me, that every one which seeth the Son, and believeth on Him, may have everlasting life; and I will raise him up at the last day" (John 6:40).

"There is therefore now no condemnation to them which are in Christ Jesus who walk not after the flesh, but after the Spirit" (Romans 8:1).

"For all the promises of God in Him are yea, and in Him Amen, unto the glory of God by us" (2 Corinthians 1:20).

PARADISE الجنّة

A Muslim friend of mine was wondering why after struggling to do good deeds, the merit was not worth it. The Islamic reward is a "paradise" garden full of physical pleasures, fruit and rivers.

"And convey good news to those who believe and do good deeds, that they shall have gardens in which rivers flow; whenever they shall be given a portion of the fruit thereof, they shall say: This is what was given to us before; and they shall be given the like of it, and they shall have pure mates (wives) in them; and in them they shall abide" (Al-Baqarah 2:25) &(Al-Imran 3:15)

وَبَشِّرِ الَّذِينَ آمَنُوا وَعَمِلُوا الصَّالِحَاتِ أَنَّ لَهُمْ جَنَّاتٍ تَجْرِي مِنْ تَحْتِهَا الْأَنْهَارُ كُلَّمَا رُزِقُوا مِنْهَا مِنْ ثَمَرَةٍ رِزْقًا قَالُوا هَذَا الَّذِي رُزِقْنَا مِنْ قَبْلُ وَأُتُوا بِهِ مُتَشَابِهًا وَلَهُمْ فِيهَا أَزْوَاجٌ مُطَهَّرَةٌ وَهُمْ فِيهَا خَالِدُونَ . البقرة 25

قُلْ أَؤُنَبِّئُكُمْ بِخَيْرٍ مِنْ ذَلِكُمْ لِلَّذِينَ اتَّقَوْا عِنْدَ رَبِّهِمْ جَنَّاتٌ تَجْرِي مِنْ تَحْتِهَا الْأَنْهَارُ خَالِدِينَ فِيهَا وَأَزْوَاجٌ مُطَهَّرَةٌ وَرِضْوَانٌ مِنَ اللَّهِ وَاللَّهُ بَصِيرٌ بِالْعِبَادِ .

ال عمران 15

THE TRUTH OF THE QURA'N IN THE LIGHT OF THE BIBLE

"...And you shall have therein what your souls desire, and you shall have therein what you ask for" (Al-Sajdah, Faslat, 41:31).

نَحْنُ أَوْلِيَاؤُكُمْ فِي الْحَيَاةِ الدُّنْيَا وَفِي الْآخِرَةِ وَلَكُمْ فِيهَا مَا تَشْتَهِي أَنْفُسُكُمْ وَلَكُمْ فِيهَا مَا تَدَّعُونَ . فصلت 31

"...In them shall be those who restrained their eyes, before them neither man nor jinn (spirits) shall have touched them..." (Al-Rahman 55:478-7).

فَبِأَيِّ آلَاءِ رَبِّكُمَا تُكَذِّبَانِ (47) ذَوَاتَا أَفْنَانٍ (48) فَبِأَيِّ آلَاءِ رَبِّكُمَا تُكَذِّبَانِ (49) فِيهِمَا عَيْنَانِ تَجْرِيَانِ (50) فَبِأَيِّ آلَاءِ رَبِّكُمَا تُكَذِّبَانِ (51) فِيهِمَا مِنْ كُلِّ فَاكِهَةٍ زَوْجَانِ (52) فَبِأَيِّ آلَاءِ رَبِّكُمَا تُكَذِّبَانِ (53) مُتَّكِئِينَ عَلَى فُرُشٍ بَطَائِنُهَا مِنْ إِسْتَبْرَقٍ وَجَنَى الْجَنَّتَيْنِ دَانٍ (54) فَبِأَيِّ آلَاءِ رَبِّكُمَا تُكَذِّبَانِ (55) فِيهِنَّ قَاصِرَاتُ الطَّرْفِ لَمْ يَطْمِثْهُنَّ إِنْسٌ قَبْلَهُمْ وَلَا جَانٌّ (56) فَبِأَيِّ آلَاءِ رَبِّكُمَا تُكَذِّبَانِ (57) كَأَنَّهُنَّ الْيَاقُوتُ وَالْمَرْجَانُ (58) فَبِأَيِّ آلَاءِ رَبِّكُمَا تُكَذِّبَانِ (59) هَلْ جَزَاءُ الْإِحْسَانِ إِلَّا الْإِحْسَانُ (60) فَبِأَيِّ آلَاءِ رَبِّكُمَا تُكَذِّبَانِ (61) وَمِنْ دُونِهِمَا جَنَّتَانِ (62) فَبِأَيِّ آلَاءِ رَبِّكُمَا تُكَذِّبَانِ (63) مُدْهَامَّتَانِ (64) فَبِأَيِّ آلَاءِ رَبِّكُمَا تُكَذِّبَانِ (65) فِيهِمَا عَيْنَانِ نَضَّاخَتَانِ (66) فَبِأَيِّ آلَاءِ رَبِّكُمَا تُكَذِّبَانِ (67) فِيهِمَا فَاكِهَةٌ وَنَخْلٌ وَرُمَّانٌ (68) فَبِأَيِّ آلَاءِ رَبِّكُمَا تُكَذِّبَانِ (69) فِيهِنَّ خَيْرَاتٌ حِسَانٌ (70) فَبِأَيِّ آلَاءِ رَبِّكُمَا تُكَذِّبَانِ (71) حُورٌ مَقْصُورَاتٌ فِي الْخِيَامِ (72) فَبِأَيِّ آلَاءِ رَبِّكُمَا تُكَذِّبَانِ (73) لَمْ يَطْمِثْهُنَّ إِنْسٌ قَبْلَهُمْ وَلَا جَانٌّ (74) فَبِأَيِّ آلَاءِ رَبِّكُمَا تُكَذِّبَانِ (75) مُتَّكِئِينَ عَلَى رَفْرَفٍ خُضْرٍ وَعَبْقَرِيٍّ حِسَانٍ (76) فَبِأَيِّ آلَاءِ رَبِّكُمَا تُكَذِّبَانِ (77) تَبَارَكَ اسْمُ رَبِّكَ ذِي الْجَلَالِ وَالْإِكْرَامِ (78) . 47-78 الرحمن

"And with them shall be those who restrain the eyes, having beautiful eyes; as if they were eggs carefully protected…A speaker from among them shall say: Surely I had a comrade of mine." Al-Safat 37:42-48)

فَوَاكِهُ وَهُمْ مُكْرَمُونَ (42) فِي جَنَّاتِ النَّعِيمِ (43) عَلَى سُرُرٍ مُتَقَابِلِينَ (44) يُطَافُ عَلَيْهِمْ بِكَأْسٍ مِنْ مَعِينٍ (45) بَيْضَاءَ لَذَّةٍ لِلشَّارِبِينَ (46) لَا فِيهَا غَوْلٌ وَلَا هُمْ عَنْهَا يُنْزَفُونَ (47) وَعِنْدَهُمْ قَاصِرَاتُ الطَّرْفِ عِينٌ (48) كَأَنَّهُنَّ بَيْضٌ مَكْنُونٌ . الصافات 42-48

"And We will aid them with fruit and flesh such as they desire. They shall pass therein from one to another a cup wherein there shall be nothing vain nor any sin" (Al-Tur 52:17-24).

إِنَّ الْمُتَّقِينَ فِي جَنَّاتٍ وَنَعِيمٍ (17) فَاكِهِينَ بِمَا أَتَاهُمْ رَبُّهُمْ وَوَقَاهُمْ رَبُّهُمْ عَذَابَ الْجَحِيمِ (18) كُلُوا وَاشْرَبُوا هَنِيئًا بِمَا كُنْتُمْ تَعْمَلُونَ (19) مُتَّكِئِينَ عَلَى سُرُرٍ مَصْفُوفَةٍ وَزَوَّجْنَاهُمْ بِحُورٍ عِينٍ (20) وَالَّذِينَ آمَنُوا وَاتَّبَعَتْهُمْ ذُرِّيَّتُهُمْ بِإِيمَانٍ أَلْحَقْنَا بِهِمْ ذُرِّيَّتَهُمْ وَمَا أَلَتْنَاهُمْ مِنْ عَمَلِهِمْ مِنْ شَيْءٍ كُلُّ امْرِئٍ بِمَا كَسَبَ رَهِينٌ (21) وَأَمْدَدْنَاهُمْ بِفَاكِهَةٍ وَلَحْمٍ مِمَّا يَشْتَهُونَ (22) يَتَنَازَعُونَ فِيهَا كَأْسًا لَا لَغْوٌ فِيهَا وَلَا تَأْثِيمٌ (23) وَيَطُوفُ عَلَيْهِمْ غِلْمَانٌ لَهُمْ كَأَنَّهُمْ لُؤْلُؤٌ مَكْنُونٌ .

الطور 17-24

How can a Holy God live in such a place where evil is still present? Evil cannot live side by side with God. "Thou art of purer eyes than to behold evil, and canst not look on iniquity" (Habakkuk 1:13).

The Place of God's Holiness

What a difference there is in the Biblical heaven.

> "But as it is written, 'Eye hath not seen nor ear heard, neither have entered into the heart of man, the things which God hath prepared for them that love Him'" (1 Corinthians 2:9).

> The Apostle Paul says: "I knew a man in Christ...How that he was caught up into paradise, and heard unspeakable words, which it is not lawful for a man to utter" (2 Corinthians 12:2-4).

> "And as we have borne the image of the earthly, we shall also bear the image of the heavenly" (1 Corinthians 15:49).

"For in the resurrection they neither marry, nor are given in marriage, but are as the angels of God in heaven" (Matthew 22:30).

"And I saw a new heaven and a new earth: for the first heaven and the first earth were passed away...And I heard a great voice out of heaven saying, 'Behold, the tabernacle of God is with men, and He will dwell with them, and they shall be His people, and God Himself shall be with them, and be their God...But the fearful, and unbelieving, and the abominable, and murders, and whoremongers, and sorcerers, and idolaters, and all liars, shall have their part in the lake which burneth with fire and brimstone which is the second death'" (Revelation 21:1,3,8).

"And they shall see His face; and His name shall be in their foreheads. And there shall be no night there; and they need no candle, neither light of the sun; for the Lord God giveth them light: and they shall reign forever and ever" (Revelation 22:4-5).

WOMEN النساء

We live in a world that cries out for liberty for women and for their equality with men. People realize that monogamy is far better for a close-knit family than polygamy. Divorce without reason and lack of birth-control leads to instability. The Quranic teaching about women is largely implicative, and many Muslim scholars try to paraphrase it to suit society. The following verses from the Quran confirm its basic teaching about a woman's position.

1. <u>Marriage</u>: "If ye fear that ye shall not be able to deal justly with the orphans, marry women of your own desire: two or three or four" (Al-Nisa 4:3).

    وَإِنْ خِفْتُمْ أَلَّا تُقْسِطُوا فِي الْيَتَامَىٰ فَانكِحُوا مَا طَابَ لَكُم مِّنَ النِّسَاءِ مَثْنَىٰ وَثُلَاثَ وَرُبَاعَ ۖ فَإِنْ خِفْتُمْ أَلَّا تَعْدِلُوا فَوَاحِدَةً أَوْ مَا مَلَكَتْ أَيْمَانُكُمْ ۚ ذَٰلِكَ أَدْنَىٰ أَلَّا تَعُولُوا .
    النساء 3

2. <u>Treating wives</u>: "The male has the equal of the portion of two females" (Al-Nisa 4:11).

وَلَكُمْ نِصْفُ مَا تَرَكَ أَزْوَاجُكُمْ إِنْ لَمْ يَكُنْ لَهُنَّ وَلَدٌ فَإِنْ كَانَ لَهُنَّ وَلَدٌ فَلَكُمُ الرُّبُعُ مِمَّا تَرَكْنَ مِنْ بَعْدِ وَصِيَّةٍ يُوصِينَ بِهَا أَوْ دَيْنٍ وَلَهُنَّ الرُّبُعُ مِمَّا تَرَكْتُمْ إِنْ لَمْ يَكُنْ لَكُمْ وَلَدٌ فَإِنْ كَانَ لَكُمْ وَلَدٌ فَلَهُنَّ الثُّمُنُ مِمَّا تَرَكْتُمْ مِنْ بَعْدِ وَصِيَّةٍ تُوصُونَ بِهَا أَوْ دَيْنٍ وَإِنْ كَانَ رَجُلٌ يُورَثُ كَلَالَةً أَوِ امْرَأَةٌ وَلَهُ أَخٌ أَوْ أُخْتٌ فَلِكُلِّ وَاحِدٍ مِنْهُمَا السُّدُسُ فَإِنْ كَانُوا أَكْثَرَ مِنْ ذَلِكَ فَهُمْ شُرَكَاءُ فِي الثُّلُثِ مِنْ بَعْدِ وَصِيَّةٍ يُوصَى بِهَا أَوْ دَيْنٍ غَيْرَ مُضَارٍّ وَصِيَّةً مِنَ اللَّهِ وَاللَّهُ عَلِيمٌ حَلِيمٌ . النساء 11

"...Admonish those of them on whose part you apprehend disobedience, and leave them alone in their beds and chastise them (beat them)" (Al-Nisa 4:34).

الرِّجَالُ قَوَّامُونَ عَلَى النِّسَاءِ بِمَا فَضَّلَ اللَّهُ بَعْضَهُمْ عَلَى بَعْضٍ وَبِمَا أَنْفَقُوا مِنْ أَمْوَالِهِمْ فَالصَّالِحَاتُ قَانِتَاتٌ حَافِظَاتٌ لِلْغَيْبِ بِمَا حَفِظَ اللَّهُ وَاللَّاتِي تَخَافُونَ نُشُوزَهُنَّ فَعِظُوهُنَّ وَاهْجُرُوهُنَّ فِي الْمَضَاجِعِ وَاضْرِبُوهُنَّ فَإِنْ أَطَعْنَكُمْ فَلَا تَبْغُوا عَلَيْهِنَّ سَبِيلًا إِنَّ اللَّهَ كَانَ عَلِيًّا كَبِيرًا . النساء 34

"And if you desire to take a wife in place of another and you have given one of them a treasure, take not back aught therefrom" (Al-Nisa 4:20).

وَإِنْ أَرَدْتُمُ اسْتِبْدَالَ زَوْجٍ مَكَانَ زَوْجٍ وَآتَيْتُمْ إِحْدَاهُنَّ قِنْطَارًا فَلَا تَأْخُذُوا مِنْهُ شَيْئًا أَتَأْخُذُونَهُ بُهْتَانًا وَإِثْمًا مُبِينًا . النساء 20

3. <u>Divorce</u>: "There is no blame on you if you divorce women when you have not touched them or appointed for them a portion" (Al-Baqarah 2:236).

لَا جُنَاحَ عَلَيْكُمْ إِنْ طَلَّقْتُمُ النِّسَاءَ مَا لَمْ تَمَسُّوهُنَّ أَوْ تَفْرِضُوا لَهُنَّ فَرِيضَةً وَمَتِّعُوهُنَّ عَلَى الْمُوسِعِ قَدَرُهُ وَعَلَى الْمُقْتِرِ قَدَرُهُ مَتَاعًا بِالْمَعْرُوفِ حَقًّا عَلَى الْمُحْسِنِينَ . البقرة 236

"And if you divorce them before you have touched them and you have appointed for them a portion, then (pay to them) half of what you have appointed" (Al-Baqarah 2:237).

وَإِنْ طَلَّقْتُمُوهُنَّ مِنْ قَبْلِ أَنْ تَمَسُّوهُنَّ وَقَدْ فَرَضْتُمْ لَهُنَّ فَرِيضَةً فَنِصْفُ مَا فَرَضْتُمْ إِلَّا أَنْ يَعْفُونَ أَوْ يَعْفُوَ الَّذِي بِيَدِهِ عُقْدَةُ النِّكَاحِ وَأَنْ تَعْفُوا أَقْرَبُ لِلتَّقْوَى وَلَا تَنْسَوُا الْفَضْلَ بَيْنَكُمْ إِنَّ اللَّهَ بِمَا تَعْمَلُونَ بَصِيرٌ . البقرة 237

4. <u>Re-marriage</u>: "So if he divorce her, she shall not be lawful to him afterwards until she marries another husband: then if he divorce her, there is no blame on them both if they return to each other" (Al-Baqarah 2:230).

فَإِنْ طَلَّقَهَا فَلَا تَحِلُّ لَهُ مِنْ بَعْدُ حَتَّى تَنْكِحَ زَوْجًا غَيْرَهُ فَإِنْ طَلَّقَهَا فَلَا جُنَاحَ عَلَيْهِمَا أَنْ يَتَرَاجَعَا إِنْ ظَنَّا أَنْ يُقِيمَا حُدُودَ اللَّهِ وَتِلْكَ حُدُودُ اللَّهِ يُبَيِّنُهَا لِقَوْمٍ يَعْلَمُونَ البقرة 230

Compare the difference in the Biblical teaching. Here are a few verses from the Bible.

1. <u>Marriage</u>: "For this cause shall a man leave his father and mother, and shall be joined unto his wife, and they two shall be one flesh" (Ephesians 5:31).

   "Marriage is honourable in all, and the bed undefiled" (Hebrews 13:4).

2. <u>Treating women</u>: "Likewise, ye husbands, dwell with them according to knowledge, giving honour unto the wife, as unto the weaker vessel, and being heirs together of the grace of life; that your prayers be not unhindered" (1 Peter 3:7).

   "…the elder women as mothers; the younger as sisters, with all purity" (1 Timothy 5:2).

   "Nevertheless, let everyone of you in particular so love his wife, even as himself" (Ephesians 5:33).

"...That whosoever looketh on a woman to lust after her hath committed adultery with her already in his heart" (Matthew 5:28).

3. <u>Divorce</u>: "But I say unto you, that whosoever shall put away his wife, saving for the cause of fornication, causeth her to commit adultery..." (Matthew 5:32).

"But from the beginning of the creation God made them male and female...What therefore God hath joined together, let not man put asunder" (Mark 10:6,9).

4. <u>Remarriage</u>: "And I say unto you, Whosoever shall put away his wife, except it be for fornication, and shall marry another, committeth adultery: and whoso marrieth her which is put away doth commit adultery" (Matthew 19:9).

THE EXCELLENCY OF THE BIBLE

معجزة الكتاب المقدس

It is only in recent years that the Quran has been translated into a few languages, as Muslims believed that the original Arabic language that Allah sent the Quran in, the language of Allah and Heaven, should not be translated. "…And this is a book in Arabic…" (Al-Ahqaf 46:12).

وَمِنْ قَبْلِهِ كِتَابُ مُوسَى إِمَامًا وَرَحْمَةً وَهَذَا كِتَابٌ مُصَدِّقٌ لِسَانًا عَرَبِيًّا لِيُنْذِرَ الَّذِينَ ظَلَمُوا وَبُشْرَى لِلْمُحْسِنِينَ . الاحقاف 12

It has been said that the excellency of the Quran was due to the fact that "you cannot understand everything"! In fact, the words are often incomprehensible. Yet how can man obey God's commandments if he does not understand what God is trying to say to him?

It is because of God's love that He has given us His laws in a manner that we can comprehend. He has used holy men moved by

His Holy Spirit to write the Bible in ways that can be understood. "For the prophecy came not in old time by the will of man: but holy men of God spake as they were moved by the Holy Ghost" (2 Peter 1:21).

There has never been a problem through the centuries in the translation of the Bible. This is the miracle and the excellency of the Bible.

The Ultimate Love

This is the uttermost example of God's love, that He should open the door widely for mankind to understand Him, to come to Him, and to ask His forgiveness. "But God commendeth His love towards us, in that while we were yet sinners, Christ died for us" (Romans 5:8).

So He sent His own Word, Jesus Christ, to dwell in the flesh, and to reconcile us to Himself. "For if when we were enemies, we were reconciled to God by the death of His Son, much more, being reconciled, we shall be saved by His life" (Romans 5:10).

For such a relationship with God was first severed by Adam's sin, and then by ours as well. What shall I do, then? I must first see that I, too, have fallen short of the goodness and perfection that is in God. "For all have sinned, and come short of the glory of God" (Romans 3:23)

I must recognize that I deserve God's punishment, because in my heart, I cannot love the way He loves. I cannot obey His righteous laws without making many errors. No matter how many good works I have done, how much I have prayed, I still have no power to change my heart. I have no way to cleanse my conscience from the guilt that divides me from my Creator and Lord, as hard as I might try.

God's Word is true, and it stirs my heart to respond as I see the vast difference between myself and Him. He truly knows the secrets of my heart that no man can know. "For the Word of God is quick, and powerful, and sharper than any two-edged sword, piercing even to the dividing asunder of soul and spirit, and of the joint and marrow, and is a discerner of the thoughts and intents of the heart" (Hebrews 4:12).

Confronted by the love of a holy God, if we are honest about understanding the obvious consequences, we are left to confess that without His mercy, we are truly helpless. "For the wages of sin is death…" (Romans 6:23) "O wretched man that I am! Who shall deliver me from the body of this death?" (Romans 7:24).

How Can it Be?

As quickly as I perceive my desperate need for forgiveness, the Lord Jesus is ever quick to respond to my need with hope. As God in heaven, as the One who knows the thoughts and prayers of my heart, "He is not far from every one of us" (Acts 17:27).

He is near to all who call on His name, to give the gift of eternal life that He purchased for us at the cross, paying the debt for every man, woman and child. "He commendeth His love towards us, in that, while we were yet sinners, Christ died for us" (Romans

5:8). "He came not to judge the world, but to save the world" (John 12:47).

A Gift for All

Beloved of God, this gift is for you. "For God so loved the world, that He gave His only begotten Son, that whosoever believeth in Him should not perish, but have everlasting life" (John 3:16).

Like a shepherd calls to his flock, Jesus calls us to Himself, to find water for our souls and balm for the wounds of our hearts.

"Come unto me, all ye that labor and are heavy laden, and I will give you rest" (Matthew 11:28). "I have loved thee with an everlasting love, therefore with loving kindness have I drawn thee" (Jeremiah 31:3). "Him that cometh to me, I will in no wise cast out" (John 6:37).

He is fully willing to save, and our response of faith is of greater value to Him than any offering of our hands or flesh. "A man is justified by faith without the deeds of the law" (Romans 3:28). "For by grace are ye saved through faith, and that not of yourselves; it is the gift of God, not of works, lest any man should boast" (Ephesians 2:8-9).

So our response to God's offer is to repent of our sins. "If we confess our sins, He is faithful and just to forgive our sins, and to cleanse us from all unrighteousness" (1 John 1:9). In a humble prayer, yield your heart to the Lord Jesus Christ, and commit your life to His care. Ask Him to reveal His truth to you, to fill you with His Spirit and teach you His ways.

A New Day

He knows the paths we have traveled, and brings us today to a new place. "The time of this ignorance God winked at, but now commandeth all men everywhere to repent" (Acts 17:30).

We may stand in full assurance and confidence that when such confession is made, we do belong to the God of heaven, and His Spirit has entered our lives to both cleanse and to give us the power to walk with Him in His love. "There is therefore now no condemnation to them which are in Christ Jesus, who walk not after the flesh, but after the Spirit" (Romans 8:1).

New life in Christ is a life of peace with God and within ourselves. "Blessed is he whose transgression is forgiven, whose sin is covered" (Psalms 32:1). "Therefore being justified by faith, we have peace with God through our Lord Jesus Christ" (Romans 5:1). It is a peace to be enjoyed here in this mortal life, and eternally with God in heaven.

Friend, do not reject such a great gift! "Today if ye will hear His voice, harden not your hearts…" (Hebrews 3:7-8). "Thou art inexcusable, O man" (Romans 2:1). "The light is come into the world" (John 3:19).

Do not wait, if the Spirit of God has revealed to you His truth. Will you receive it today? If doubts dismay you, call on the name of the Lord Jesus to show you the Truth Himself.

Jesus said: "I am the way, the truth, and the life, no man cometh unto the Father but by me." (John 14:6)

قَالَ يَسُوعُ:

"أَنَا هُوَ الطَّرِيقُ وَالْحَقُّ وَالْحَيَاةُ. لَيْسَ أَحَدٌ يَأْتِي إِلَى الآبِ إِلاَّ بِي".

الانجيل بحسب القديس يوحنا 14: 6